PENGUIN BOOKS

THE LANGUAGE OF THE GARDEN

Anne Scott-James has had two lifelong passions – gardening and the meaning of words. Her first garden was a radish-and-daisy plot at St Paul's Girls' School, where her special subject was classics. She won a classical scholarship to Somerville College, Oxford, and after Oxford went into journalism, writing features for *Picture Post*, then a weekly page for the *Sunday Express*, and later a column on current affairs for the *Daily Mail*. She extended her interest in words into radio and was a panellist on *My Word!* for thirteen years. She now specializes in garden writing and is the author of many books including *Down to Earth*, *Sissinghurst*, *The Cottage Garden* and *The Pleasure Garden*, the last illustrated by her husband, Osbert Lancaster. She has a cottage with an old-fashioned garden on the Berkshire downs.

ANNE SCOTT-JAMES

The
Language of the
Garden

A Personal Anthology

PENGUIN BOOKS

Penguin Books Ltd, 27 Wrights Lane, London w8 5TZ (Publishing and Editorial)
and Harmondsworth, Middlesex, England (Distribution and Warehouse)
Viking Penguin Inc., 40 West 23rd Street, New York, New York 10010, USA
Penguin Books Australia Ltd, Ringwood, Victoria, Australia
Penguin Books Canada Ltd, 2801 John Street, Markham, Ontario, Canada L3R 1B4
Penguin Books (NZ) Ltd, 182–190 Wairau Road, Auckland 10, New Zealand

First published by Viking 1984
Published in Penguin Books 1987

Copyright © Anne Scott-James, 1984
The acknowlegements on pp. 245–8 constitute an extension of this copyright page
All rights reserved

Set in VIP Garamond

Reproduced, printed and bound in Great Britain by
Hazell Watson & Viney Limited,
Member of the BPCC Group,
Aylesbury, Bucks

For Calypso

TO THE READER

Happy art thou, whom God does bless
With the full choice of thine own happiness . . .
    In books and gardens thou has plac'd aright . . .
Thy noble, innocent delight.

ABRAHAM COWLEY,
The Garden

CONTENTS

LIST OF ILLUSTRATIONS

Title page: illustration by Osbert Lancaster in Anne Scott-James, *Down to Earth* (1971)

INTRODUCTION

Gardening and reading go together as naturally as eggs and bacon, and I have enjoyed both activities all my life. Gardens have, from the beginning, inspired miracles of literature. We read with awe of gardens of sacred or profane love, gardens of death, gardens for contemplation, gardens for God's vengeance. But, thank heaven, gardening is a source of comedy, too, and gardens of absurdity, idleness, jealousy or mishap have been neatly recorded by ironic, or even waspish, pens. Didactic gardening books can also give pleasure, raising Walter Mitty dreams of luxuriant flowers and delicious things to eat in one's own domain. Since gardeners experience a wide range of emotions as they go about their work, from ecstasy when a rare plant blooms to rage at a visiting rabbit, they respond readily to many different kinds of garden literature. One can enjoy the Song of Solomon or Pope, Tennyson or *The Diary of a Nobody*, according to one's mood.

My book makes no claim to be comprehensive, but is a personal choice, and I hope that readers will forgive me if I have failed to include some of their favourite authors.

The
Language of the Garden

There is no place like a garden, with its assault on all the senses, for intensifying human emotion, and stirring writers to extremes of happiness or woe. I open this collection with two poems of passion, one a dream of sensual joy, the other a black comedy.

Tennyson's poem is surely one of the most beautiful in the English language. It is best read in an anthology, away from its unfortunate environment, the silly story of the Princess Ida who founded a university for women. The Princess is (as Gilbert and Sullivan discovered) full of risible incidents, as when the lovesick Prince and his two courtiers gain access to the university by dressing in drag; but it is jewelled with glorious lyrics, such as 'The splendour falls on castle walls' and this deeply sexual poem of lovers in a garden at nightfall.

Now sleeps the crimson petal, now the white;
Nor waves the cypress in the palace walk;
Nor winks the gold fin in the porphyry font:
The fire-fly wakens: waken thou with me.

Now droops the milkwhite peacock like a ghost,
And like a ghost she glimmers on to me.

Now lies the Earth all Danaë to the stars,
And all thy heart lies open unto me.

Now slides the silent meteor on, and leaves
A shining furrow, as thy thoughts in me.

Now folds the lily all her sweetness up,
And slips into the bosom of the lake:
So fold thyself, my dearest, thou, and slip
Into my bosom and be lost in me.

ALFRED LORD TENNYSON,
The Princess, 1847

John Donne's poem Twicknam Garden *is a sardonic record of frustrated passion.*

Blasted with sighs, and surrounded with teares,
    Hither I come to seeke the spring,
    And at mine eyes, and at mine eares,
Receive such balmes, as else cure every thing;
    But O, selfe traytor, I do bring
The spider love, which transubstantiates all,
    And can convert Manna to gall,
And that this place may thoroughly be thought
    True Paradise, I have the serpent brought.

'Twere wholsomer for mee, that winter did
    Benight the glory of this place,
    And that a grave frost did forbid
These trees to laugh, and mocke mee to my face;
    But that I may not this disgrace
Indure, nor yet leave loving, Love let mee
    Some senslesse peece of this place bee;
Make me a mandrake, so I may groane here.
    Or a stone fountaine weeping out my yeare.

Hither with christall vyals, lovers come,
    And take my teares, which are loves wine,
    And try your mistresse Teares at home,
For all are false, that tast not just like mine;
    Alas, hearts do not in eyes shine,
Nor can you more judge womans thoughts by
      teares,
    Than by her shadow, what she weares.

O perverse sexe, where none is true but shee,
Who's therefore true, because her truth kills me.

JOHN DONNE,
Twicknam Garden, early 17th century

One of the most encouraging things about gardening is that, though money helps, it is nothing like as important as green fingers. Often, rich men make hideous gardens and poor, uneducated men have the innate taste and skill to grow finer crops and lovelier flowers than all their neighbours. If I could meet just one great gardener of the past, I think I would choose Virgil's old man who was a native of Corycus, in Asia Minor, but who was gardening in old age in Southern Italy. Endowed with the greenest of green fingers, I feel sure he would have given me cuttings and seeds and a share of his knowledge.

I remember seeing, under the towers of the citadel of Oebalia, where the black river Galasus waters the yellow fields, an old man from Corycus who owned a few acres of derelict land. The soil was not rich enough to plough, nor good for grazing, nor suitable for vines. Yet here among the scrub he planted vegetables, and white lilies round about, and vervain and fragile poppies, and he felt himself to be as rich as a king, and, returning home late in the evening, would load his board with home-grown delicacies.

He was the first to pick roses in spring and apples in autumn, and, when gloomy winter was still cracking the stones with frost and checking the flow of waters with ice, he was already cutting tender hyacinths, scolding the late summer and the loitering west wind. He was also the first to enjoy productive bees and a good swarm, and the first to squeeze the combs and collect foaming honey. His limes and pines were fertile, and all the early flowers with which the trees decked themselves in spring set into autumn fruit. He planted out rows of well-grown elms and mature pear-trees and fruit-bearing plums, and also a plane-tree which was already providing drinkers with a welcome shade.

VIRGIL,
Georgics, Book IV

Shakespeare, so lyrical about wild flowers, wrote surprisingly rarely about garden flowers, and then used them to point a moral. The lilies he knew would have been madonna lilies.

The Summer's flower is to the summer sweet,
Though to itself it only live and die,
But if that flower with base infection meet,
The basest weed outbraves his dignity:
  For sweetest things turn sourest by their deeds;
  Lilies that fester smell far worse than weeds.

WILLIAM SHAKESPEARE,
Sonnet 94

Moving from the sublime to the language of hard-headed realism, I find Professor John Carey's attitude highly sympathetic. When I read his article on 'The Pleasures of Vegetable Gardening' a few years ago, I wrote him a fan letter. He replied that mine was the only letter of approval he had received. His postbox overflowed with letters of protest from cat lovers, friends of the environment, humanists, the Welsh (he was unkind about leeks), and also, if I remember aright, from pacifists, race relations specialists, women's libbers and proponents of proportional representation. This excerpt caused particular annoyance.

In this situation the only adequate response is to thank God for chemical pesticides, and use them liberally. Unfortunately the strongest and most effective ones keep being withdrawn from the market on the grounds that they have been found to damage the environment. So when you hit on a really lethal sort it's a good plan to buy it in large supply, which will allow you to go on using it after it has been outlawed. I did this for several seasons with a splendid product, now alas unobtainable, which wiped out everything from snails to flea beetles. It had no adverse effect on the bird population so far as I could see, though the neighbourhood cats did start to look a bit seedy. That, of course, was an advantage from my point of view, for cats are filthy, insanitary beasts, and a fearful nuisance to the gardener. One of the anomalies of English law is that whereas it would, as I understand it, be an offence to clamber over your neighbour's fence and defecate among his vegetables, you can send a feline accomplice on precisely the same errand with total impunity. It has always amazed me that manufacturers of slug bait, and other such garden aids, should proudly announce on the label that their product is 'harmless to pets'. A pesticide that could guarantee to cause pets irreparable damage would, I'd have thought, sell like hot cakes.

JOHN CAREY,
'The Pleasures of Vegetable Gardening', *The Sunday Times*, 1980

There is a quiet, sad note of irony which I like in this little quote from a novel by Barbara Pym. Poor Rowena, who enjoyed putting flowers casually into jugs and vases, was so easily defeated by the pundits of the Flower Arranging Movement.

'We've been having lectures on flower arrangement at the Women's Institute,' said Rowena. 'I discovered that I've been doing mine wrong for years. My arrangements, which I always thought so pretty, had no interesting focal point! Now I'm so humiliated and discouraged that I feel I'd rather have nothing at all or just plants in pots that arrange themselves.'

BARBARA PYM,
A Glass of Blessings, 1958

One understands Rowena's difficulties with the focal point when one reads the experts.

A simple and economical arrangement of spring flowers can be made with three daffodils, three tulips and a few 'pussy-willow' twigs . . .
    This arrangement is made in a flat dish or bowl, and needs a 2½″ diameter pinholder. The dish or bowl should have a water depth of at least 1½″ so that the stems of flowers when fixed in the pinholder are well in the water . . .
    The bowl or dish must be perfectly dry — slightly warmed is an advantage. The pinholder should be fixed in the required position, centrally or off-centre as desired, with *Plasticine* or *Oasis Fix* stuck to the inside of the container. The pinholder is then pressed firmly on to this adhesive. A dome of crumpled wire-netting placed over the pinholder gives an additional support for the stems . . .
    To do this arrangement I recommend that you first position centrally in the pinholder the longest twig of pussy-willow — about 1′ 6″ long . . . Note that the three longest pieces produce a triangle, the tallest just offset from the vertical and the lowest nearly horizontal. The shortest pussy-willow twig . . . on the right is added later. Now select the best and least open of your three tulips, from which it may be necessary to remove the top leaf if this is situated too near the bloom. Remember at all times that leaves not required should be carefully removed as they may be very useful later on. This first tulip, . . . about 12″ long, is placed just behind the longest twig leaning back very slightly. This gives depth to the arrangement and tends to accentuate the 'third dimension'. In front of this first tulip place your second, . . . about 9″ long, at an angle of about 45 degrees to the right and leaning slightly forward. Now add a daffodil about 9″ long, . . . positioned as shown, and looking from front to back, in between the two tulips you have just fixed. Add another daffodil, . . . about 6″ long, leaning slightly forward on the same plane as the second tulip, but to the left of the centre line. Behind

this is added your third daffodil, . . . about 10" long. The remaining piece of pussy-willow is added between the shorter, second tulip . . . and the second daffodil, . . . also leaning slightly forward. Tulip or any other suitable foliage is now added to give you a base, or frame, and all you have to do to complete the arrangement is to add the focal point. In this case it will be an opened tulip.

ERIC ROBERTS,
Teach Yourself Flower Arrangement

For Shirley Hibberd, flowers in the house created no mathematical anxieties, just pure happiness; he enjoyed bunches of wild flowers and grasses when sophisticated flowers were not to hand. His charming book about ferns, window gardens, aquaria and other living indoor decorations was immensely popular in Victorian times, and has been widely read ever since.

So many are the social qualities of flowers that it would be a difficult task to enumerate them. We always feel welcome when, on entering a room, we find a display of flowers on the table. Where there are flowers about, the hostess appears glad, the children pleased, the very dog and cat grateful for our arrival, the whole scene and all the personages seem more hearty, homely, and beautiful, because of the bewitching roses, and orchids, and lilies, and mignonette!

SHIRLEY HIBBERD,
Rustic Adornments for Homes of Taste, 1856

It may seem sacrilege not to have opened this anthology with the Garden of Eden, but the description in the Book of Genesis is somewhat skimpy. There is not even mention of an apple-tree, and those of us who assume that Eve handed Adam an apple are either confusing the Fall with the Judgement of Paris, or have seen too many Renaissance pictures with Adam and Eve under an apple-tree; the tree of life was probably, scholars say, a date-palm. This is all that the Bible tells us.

And the Lord God planted a garden eastward in Eden; and there he put the man whom he had formed.

And out of the ground made the Lord God to grow every tree that is pleasant to the sight, and good for food; the tree of life also in the midst of the garden, and the tree of knowledge of good and evil.

And a river went out of Eden to water the garden; and from thence it was parted, and became into four heads.

Genesis, II

The first detailed account of a beautiful and productive garden is to be found in Homer. The garden of Alcinous, the hospitable king of Phaeacia whom Odysseus visited on the last lap of his stormy voyage home to Ithaca, was rich in the luxuries of a hot, dry country. There was abundance of fruit, vines for wine, and spring water, and all had the magical quality of being perpetual.

Outside the courtyard, near the entrance gates, is a great garden of four acres with a fence running round on either side. Here grow tall flourishing fruit-trees: pears, pomegranates and shining apples, sweet figs and luxuriant olives. The fruit of these trees never dies off or fails, but is there winter and summer, all the year round; for the west wind, always blowing, forms new fruits even while it ripens others. Pear after pear comes to maturity, and apple after apple, one bunch of grapes after another, and fig after fig. There, too, a fruitful vineyard has been planted, of which one part, in a warm, level spot exposed to the sun, is a drying-ground, and elsewhere some grapes are being gathered, and others trodden. In front there are unripe grapes only now shedding their blossom, while others are already turning colour. There, too, beyond the furthest row of vines, are well-kept beds of herbs which are fresh all the year round, and there are two springs, one of which sprinkles the whole garden, while the other is channelled under the entrance of the courtyard to issue by the lofty palace, and here the townsfolk draw their water. These were the splendid gifts of the gods in the house of Alcinous.

HOMER,
The Odyssey, Book VII

*The garden of Alcinous has inspired many translations, but I think Pope
does it best, being a great gardener himself.*

Close to the gates a spacious garden lies,
From storms defended, and inclement skies:
Four acres was th' allotted space of ground,
Fenc'd with a green enclosure all around.
Tall thriving trees confess'd the fruitful mould;
The red'ning apple ripens here to gold,
Here the blue fig with luscious juice o'erflows,
With deeper red the full pomegranate glows,
The branch here bends beneath the weighty pear,
And verdant olives flourish round the year . . .
Each dropping pear a following pear supplies,
On apples apples, figs on figs arise.

ALEXANDER POPE,
translation of the *Odyssey*, Book VII,
in the *Guardian*, 1713

I am afraid that gardens do not cleanse the soul from a desire to score over other people. Dr Johnson, of course, did not snub from unkindness, but from a love of argument, but the victims of his wit must have felt deflated all the same. Horace Walpole said of him, 'though he was good-natured at bottom, he was ill-natured at top', and the poor lady who was devoted to the Picturesque must have smarted under his sally.

The Lincolnshire lady who showed him a grotto she had been making, came off no better, as I remember: 'Would it not be a pretty cool habitation in summer, Mr Johnson?' she said. 'I think it would, Madam,' replied he, '– for a toad.'

JAMES BOSWELL,
Life of Johnson, 1781

Tennyson, too, could be contradictious in the garden, if not so crushing as Dr Johnson. William Allingham, who was a diffident man, often went to visit him in the Isle of Wight.

The view of sea and land is delectable, stretching northward across the Solent up into the New Forest. Then we went down and walked about the grounds, looking at a cedar, a huge fern, an Irish yew. The dark yew in *Maud* 'sighing for Lebanon' he got at Swainston, – Sir John Simeon's. In one place are some little arches half-covered with ivy, which I pretend to believe are meant for mock ruins. This T. repudiates. He paused at a weed of goatsbeard, saying, 'It shuts up at three.' Then we went down the garden, past a large tangled fig-tree growing in the open – 'It's like a breaking wave,' says I. 'Not in the least,' says he. Such contradictions, *from him*, are noway disagreeable.

WILLIAM ALLINGHAM,
A Diary, 1863

If I ever have to leave my cottage with its dry downland garden, I shall look for a place with a pond. For pond plants, pond life, and pond reflections are always changing, not only with the seasons, but with the light. A puff of cloud passing across a blue sky will darken the sparkle of the water and cause the water-lilies to close until the sun shines again, and the quiet reflections of willows in the water will ripple in a strong breeze.

I have been a lover of ponds ever since my childhood when I collected small frogs in a village duckpond and got covered with mud picking arrowhead and irises. But a pond must be a pond, not a lake. The late John Christie, creator of the Glyndebourne Opera, would correct any visitor who referred to the chain of ponds in the garden as a lake. 'Lakes,' he would say with his customary crispness, 'are what they have up north.'

The Japanese have always been great pond gardeners, and there is a lyrical description of a pond in winter in The Pillow Book of Sei Shōnagon, *a Japanese lady of high birth and exquisite taste who was a Lady-in-Waiting to the Empress Sadako in the tenth century. Sei Shōnagon, like all cultivated Japanese, loved nature, plants and gardens, and often went to a temple for retreat. (She was usually, however, for she was fond of the intrigues of court life, only too glad to be summoned back by the Empress.)*

DURING THE LONG RAINS IN THE FIFTH MONTH

During the long rains in the Fifth Month, there is something very moving about a place with a pond. Between the dense irises, water-oats, and other plants one can see the green of the water; and the entire garden seems to be the same green colour. One stays there all day long, gazing in contemplation at the clouded sky – oh, how moving it is!

I am always moved and delighted by places that have ponds – not only in the winter (when I love waking up to find that the water has frozen over) but at every time of the year. The ponds I like best are not those in which everything is carefully laid out; I much prefer one that has been left to itself so that it is wild and covered with weeds.

At night in the green spaces of water one can seen nothing but the pale glow of the moonlight. At any time and in any place I find moonlight very moving.

The Pillow Book of Sei Shōnagon

The English are the only nation which can rival the Japanese in their obsession with gardens. Perhaps it is because we enjoy the same sort of wet, temperate climate. But, unlike the Japanese, with their restrictive rules and symbols, the English gardener is fancy-free to create a landscape, if he has a mind to, or to build up a plant collection, or to stuff a cottage garden with sweet-smelling flowers. Richard Barnfield's poem celebrates the formal Elizabethan garden.

I have a garden plot,
 Wherein there wants nor hearbs, nor roots, nor flowers:
Flowers to smell, roots to eate, hearbs for the pot,
 And dainty shelters when the welkin lowers:
Sweet-smelling beds of lillies, and of roses,
Which rosemary banks and lavender incloses.

There growes the gillifloure, the mynt, the dayzie
 Both red and white, the blue-veynd violet;
 The purple hyacinth, the spyke to please thee,
 The scarlet dyde carnation bleeding yet:
The sage, the savery, and sweet margerum,
Isop, tyme, and eye-bright, good for the blinde and
 dumbe.

The pinke, the primrose, cowslip and daffadilly,
 The hare-bell blue, the crimson cullumbine,
Sage, lettis, parsley, and the milke-white lilly,
 The rose and speckled flowre cald sops-in-wine,
Fine pretie king-cups, and the yellow bootes,
That growes by rivers and by shallow brookes.

RICHARD BARNFIELD,
The Affectionate Shepherd, 1594

Just as English and just as attractive, though so different in scale and manner, was Horace Walpole's landscape garden at Strawberry Hill. He spent a great deal of his long life in making it, and describes it with joy in a letter to his life-long friend, Sir Horace Mann, who lived in Italy.

The enclosed enchanted little landscape, then, is Strawberry Hill; and I will try to explain so much of it to you as will help to let you know whereabouts we are when we are talking to you; for it is uncomfortable in so intimate a correspondence as ours not to be exactly master of every spot where one another is writing, or reading, or sauntering. This view of the castle is what I have just finished, and is the only side that will be at all regular. Directly before it is an open grove, through which you see a field, which is bounded by a serpentine wood of all kind of trees, and flowering shrubs, and flowers. The lawn before the house is situated on the top of a small hill, from whence to the left you see the town and church of Twickenham encircling a turn of the river, that looks exactly like a seaport in miniature. The opposite shore is a most delicious meadow, bounded by Richmond Hill, which loses itself in the noble woods of the park to the end of the prospect on the right, where is another turn of the river, and the suburbs of Kingston as luckily placed as Twickenham is on the left: and a natural terrace on the brow of my hill, with meadows of my own down to the river, commands both extremities. Is not this a tolerable prospect? You must figure that all this is perpetually enlivened by a navigation of boats and barges, and by a road below my terrace, with coaches, post-chaises, waggons, and horsemen constantly in motion, and the fields speckled with cows, horses, and sheep.

HORACE WALPOLE,
to Sir Horace Mann,
from Strawberry Hill, 1753, *Letters*, Vol. II

Though he loved the formal gardens of his time, Marvell could enjoy a wild garden, too.

I have a garden of my own,
But so with roses overgrown,
And lilies, that you would it guess
To be a little wilderness.

ANDREW MARVELL,
*The Nymph Complaining for the
Death of Her Faun, c.* 1650

Different, again, was the botanical garden of the parson-gardener-poet, the Rev. George Crabbe, as described by his son. Crabbe was an early conservationist.

In the garden, the usual foreigners gave place to the most scarce flowers, and especially to the rarer weeds, of Britain; and these were scattered here and there only for preservation . . . My father . . . passed much of his time amongst his choice weeds.

Life of the Rev. George Crabbe
by the poet's son,
also the Rev. George Crabbe, 1844

Being so varied in character, English gardening is not easy to define, but Russell Page, who has probably thought about gardening more deeply than any other modern practitioner, offers a very subtle analysis.

Processes have always given me more satisfaction than results. Perhaps this is peculiarly English and may explain our national affection for a pursuit which is always changing: growth and decay, the swing of the seasons, our inconstant weather speeding or retarding the development of a tree or the flowering and seeding of a plant. English gardens always seem to be in flux. The fugitive pleasures which gardening affords seem to be enhanced for us by a subtle and deliberate disorder that softens the emphasis of a straight line and never allows the garden to appear static or achieved.

RUSSELL PAGE,
The Education of a Gardener, 1962

Nothing could be more different than the French garden, with its avenues, waterworks and mathematical precision. 'A subtle and deliberate disorder' would have been anathema to André Le Nôtre, the greatest of French landscape architects, who began to lay out the gardens of Versailles for the Sun King in the early 1660s, a few years after his beautiful work for Nicolas Fouquet at Vaux-le-Vicomte. Horace Walpole, never pro-French, was witty in an early letter at the expense of Versailles and the King.

Stand by, clear the way, make room for the pompous appearance of Versailles le Grand! – But no: it fell so short of my idea of it, mine, that I have resigned to Gray the office of writing its panegyric. He likes it. They say I am to like it better next Sunday; when the sun is to shine, the king is to be fine, the water-works are to play, and the new knights of the Holy Ghost are to be installed! Ever since Wednesday, the day we were there, we have done nothing but dispute about it. They say, we did not see it to advantage, that we ran through the apartments, saw the garden *en passant*, and slubbered over Trianon. I say, we saw nothing. However, we had time to see that the great front is a lumber of littleness, composed of black brick, stuck full of bad old busts, and fringed with gold rails. The rooms are all small, except the great gallery, which is noble, but totally wainscoted with looking-glass. The garden is littered with statues and fountains, each of which has its tutelary deity. In particular, the elementary god of fire solaces himself in one. In another, Enceladus, in lieu of a mountain, is overwhelmed with many waters. There are avenues of water-pots, who disport themselves much in squirting up cascadelins. In short, 'tis a garden for a great child. Such was Louis Quatorze, who is here seen in his proper colours, where he commanded in person, unassisted by his armies and generals, and left to the pursuit of his own puerile ideas of glory.

HORACE WALPOLE
to Richard West Esq.,
from Paris, 1739, *Letters*, Vol. I

Saint-Simon disliked Versailles as much as did Walpole.

The gardens, which are astonishingly magnificent, but discouraging to use, are in equally bad taste. One cannot reach the freshness of the shade without passing through a torrid zone, at the end of which one has no choice but to climb and then descend a small hill, and here the gardens end. The stone path burns one's feet, but without it, one sinks into the sand and into the blackest dirt. The violence done to nature everywhere disgusts; the abundant waters, forced up and collected again, are green, thick, muddy; they shed an unhealthy and perceptible humidity, a smell which is even worse. The whole effect, which one must yet treat with respect, is incomparable, but it is something to admire, and to shun.

LE DUC DE SAINT-SIMON,
Memoirs, year 1680

However, Le Nôtre seems to have been an attractive character. He is one of the few men of whom Saint-Simon speaks nothing but good. But then Le Nôtre was not a competitor in the court intrigues.

Le Nôtre died at about this time. He had lived in perfect health for eighty-eight years and retained his faculties, excellent taste, and capability until the last. He was celebrated for designing the fine gardens that adorn all France and have so lowered the reputation of Italian gardens (which are really nothing by comparison) that the most famous landscape architects of Italy now come to France to study and admire. Le Nôtre was honest, honourable, and plain-spoken; everybody loved and respected him, for he never stepped out of his place nor forgot it and was always perfectly disinterested, working for private patrons as for the King himself, and with the same care and industry. His only thought was to aid nature and reveal true beauty at as low a cost as possible. There was an artlessness about him, a simple-hearted candour that was perfectly delightful. On one occasion, when the Pope had obtained the King's permission to borrow him for a few months, Le Nôtre entered his room, and instead of falling to his knees, ran towards him, and putting his arms round his neck kissed him on both cheeks, exclaiming, 'Ah! Holy Father, how well you look! How rejoiced I am to see you in good health!' The Pope, Clement X, Alfieri, laughed heartily. He thoroughly enjoyed this informal kind of greeting and treated Le Nôtre with much kindness.

After he returned, the King took him into the gardens of Versailles and showed him all that had been done in his absence. When they reached the colonnade, Le Nôtre did not utter a word until the King pressed him for his opinion. 'Well, Sire,' said he, 'what would you have me say? You have turned a stone-mason into a gardener [he was referring to Mansard] and he has treated you to one of the tricks of his trade.' The King said nothing and everyone smiled, for indeed, although it pretends to be one, the colonnade has little resemblance to a fountain and is vastly out of place in a garden.

A month or so before he died, the King, who enjoyed seeing and talking to him, again took him into the gardens and because of his great age had him put into a chair, which a footman wheeled beside his own. Thereupon Le Nôtre exclaimed, 'Alas! my poor father, had he but been alive to see this poor gardener, his own son, riding in a chair beside the greatest king on earth, his happiness would have been complete.'

He was superintendent of the royal residences and lived at the Tuileries, where he had charge of the palace and the gardens, which he had designed. All that he did is still considered far better than anything done since, although many have taken the greatest pains to imitate and follow him as far as they were capable. About ornamental flower-beds, he used to say that they were only good for nursemaids who were tied to their charges and could look down upon them from second-storey windows. Nevertheless, he excelled in designing them, as well as all other parts of a garden; but he did not care for them, and he was right, because no one ever walks in those parts.

LE DUC DE SAINT-SIMON,
Memoirs, year 1700

In a hot dry country the garden is more important than the flower — a well-loved garden may be just a grove of trees with a spring of water. In a temperate country like our own, flowers become increasingly significant with every century, as plant knowledge and material expand. Chaucer loved the simple gardens of his day, though, apart from roses and lilies, he knew mostly wild flowers.

> And flowers yellow, white and red,
> Such plenty grew there never in mead,
> Full gay was all the ground, and quaint
> And powdered as men had it paint.

> GEOFFREY CHAUCER,
> *The Romance of the Rose*,
> translated from the French

By John Parkinson's time England had a wonderful variety of garden flowers, including exotics from east and west. It is not going too far to say that Parkinson adored flowers. Like the rest of us, when he saw a particularly lovely flower he longed to possess it.

The anemones likewise or windflowers are so full of variety and so dainty, so pleasant and so delightsome flowers, that the sight of them doth enforce an earnest longing desire in the mind of anyone to be a possessor of some of them at the least. For without all doubt, this one kind of flower, so variable in colours, so differing in form (being almost as many sorts of them double as single), so plentiful in bearing flowers, and so durable in lasting, and also so easy both to preserve and to increase, is of itself alone almost sufficient to furnish a garden with their flowers for almost half the year.

JOHN PARKINSON,
Paradisi in Sole,
Paradisus Terrestris, 1629

Another great seventeenth-century plantsman, John Rea, talked to his flowers and thought of them as people.

Into your garden you can walk
And with each plant and flower talk;
View all their glories, from each one
Raise some rare meditation.
Recount their natures, tell which are
Vertuous like you, as well as fair.

JOHN REA,
Flora, Ceres and Pomona, 1665

*Walter Savage Landor loved flowers so unselfishly that he would not pick
them, an abstinence I myself could not emulate. I love picking flowers in the
garden and remember the joys of picking wild flowers in my youth, often to
pack them in damp moss and post them to my mother in London. Now that
this is forbidden in the interests of conservation, I feel that children are
missing a sweet and valuable part of childhood.*

And 'tis and ever was my wish and way
To let all flowers live freely, and all die
Whene'er their genius bids their soul depart,
Among their kindred in their native place.
I never pluck the rose; the violet's head
Hath shaken with my breath upon its bank
And not reproached me; the ever-sacred cup
Of the pure lily hath between my hands
Felt safe, unsoiled, nor lost one grain of gold.

WALTER SAVAGE LANDOR,
Fiesolan Idyll, 1831

Colette's adored mother, Sido, was prodigal with presents of plants and flowers, but Colette wrote in her memoir that she refused to waste them on the wrong recipients.

Sido loathed flowers to be sacrificed. Although her one idea was to give, I have seen her refuse a request for flowers to adorn a hearse or a grave. She would harden her heart, frown, and answer 'No' with a vindictive look.

'But it's for poor Monsieur Enfert who died last night! Poor Madame Enfert's so pathetic, she says if she could see her husband depart covered with flowers, it would console her! And you've got such lovely moss-roses, Madame Colette.'

'My moss-roses on a corpse! What an outrage!'

COLETTE,
Sido, 1929

Describing flowers is not at all easy. Writers fall into terrible clichés about rich fragrance, elegance of form, a charming habit of growth, and so on. But Mr Bowles always found fresh words, which is why his My Garden *trilogy has endured to become a classic. His smelly allium is now known as* Allium siculum, *and I grow it among roses to discourage greenfly.*

A curious plant grows at the corner here, *Allium dioscoridis*, often called *Nectaroscordum siculum*, a tall, strange-looking thing to be one of the Garlicks. It possesses the most pungent and evil smell of any plant I know, and I enjoy breaking a leaf in half and getting my friends to help in deciding whether it most resembles an escape of gas or a new mackintosh. It is already throwing up its curious heads of flowers; at present they are enclosed in a leafy bag looking like the bud of some very tall Narcissus. Later on they emerge, and the buds hang down and open a few at a time, but after flowering stand upright. The flowers are a shrimp pink marked with green and dull red, and are very interesting because it regularly happens that the first to open has eight perianth segments and anthers to match, the next few have the normal six of a liliaceous plant, but towards the end of the flowering it can only afford the last few flowers four each.

E. A. BOWLES,
My Garden in Spring, 1914

Mrs Earle was another who saw flowers with fresh, observant eyes.

The orange Crown Imperials do best here, so, of course, I feel proudest of the pale yellow. Both colours are unusually good this year. In my youth they were rather sniffed at and called a cottage plant. I wonder if anyone who thought them vulgar ever took the trouble to pick off one of the down-hanging bells and turn it up to see the six drops of clear water in the six white cups with black rims? I know nothing prettier or more curious amongst flowers than this.

MRS C. W. EARLE,
Pot-Pourri from a Surrey Garden, 1897

*Gardening is not all a happy fairy story. It is a hazardous activity, a
tragi-comedy with a banana-skin ever at one's feet, and one identifies and
sympathizes with the man who skids on it.*

*Fanny Burney's husband, M. d'Arblay, was a chronic skidder, and one
longs to help him. He was a French aristocrat and refugee from the French
Revolution, and as the d'Arblays had no money, after their marriage in
1793 they took to cottage life. M. d'Arblay drew up a plan for their first
garden in Surrey and tried to work it himself, but as Fanny wrote to her
father in 1794, everything went wrong. The author of* Evelina *had not lost
the comic power of her pen.*

Seeds are sowing in some parts where plants ought to be reaping,
and plants are running to seed while they are thought not yet at
maturity. Our garden, therefore, is not yet quite the most profitable
thing in the world; but Mr d'A. assures me it is to be the staff of our
table and existence.

A little, too, he has been unfortunate; for, after immense toil in
planting and transplanting strawberries round our hedge, here at
Bookham, he has just been informed they will bear no fruit the first
year, and the second we may be 'over the hills and far away!'

Another time, too, with great labour, he cleared a considerable
compartment of weeds, and when it looked clean and well, and he
showed his work to the gardener, the man said he had demolished
an asparagus bed! M. d'A. protested, however, nothing could look
more like *les mauvaises herbes*.

His greatest passion is for transplanting. Everything we possess he
moves from one end of the garden to another, to produce better
effects. Roses take place of jessamines, jessamines of honeysuckles,
and honeysuckles of lilacs, till they have all danced round as far as
the space allows . . .

Such is our horticultural history. But I must not omit that we
have had for one week cabbages from our own cultivation every day!
Oh, you have no idea how sweet they tasted! We agreed they had a

freshness and a *goût* we had never met before. We had them for too short a time to grow tired of them, because, as I have already hinted, they were beginning to run to seed before we knew they were eatable.

There is much of Mr Pooter here. This was the d'Arblays' first garden, but they had no better luck with their second. M. d'Arblay was in ecstasy at the prospect of 'cabbage walks, potato beds, bean perfumes, and peas blossoms', but the poor man was prone to disaster. Fanny reported to her father in 1796:

M. d'Arblay has worked most laboriously in his garden, but his misfortunes there, during our absence, might melt a heart of stone. The horses of our neighbouring farmer broke through our hedges, and have made a kind of bog of our meadow, by scampering in it during the wet; the sheep followed, who have eaten up all our greens, every sprout and cabbage and lettuce destined for the winter, while the horses dug up our turnips and carrots; and the swine, pursuing such examples, have trod down all the young plants, besides devouring whatever the others left of vegetables. Our potatoes, left, from our abrupt departure, in the ground, are all rotten or frost-bitten, and utterly spoilt; and not a single thing has our whole ground produced us since we came home. A few dried carrots, which remain from the indoor collection, are all we have to temper our viands.

FANNY BURNEY,
Letters

Cassandra of the Daily Mirror *was one of the great newspaper columnists of our time. His range of subjects was wide, and he was equally convincing expressing political fury or recording conversations in the local pub. An experienced gardener, he once had a terrible accident.*

A RAY OF SUNSHINE

It always surprises me how much enjoyment people can get out of other people's mishaps.

I have just given immense pleasure to many of my friends.

I have brightened their lives. I have let sunshine into dark places.

I was in the tap room of a pub noted for the fierce conversations that go on about gardening, and an acquaintance of mine, with whom I have horticultural rivalry, said:

'Growing sweet peas again this year?'

'Yes, I am – I mean, yes, I was.'

'Come again?'

'My sweet peas are strictly in the past tense.'

'Frost?'

'No, they are in the greenhouse. Or rather they were in the greenhouse.'

'What happened?'

'I watered them with liquid weed-killer.'

'Pray say that again.'

'I watered them with a can that had contained weed-killer.'

A roar of pure delight shook the pub.

'Intentionally?'

'No, you great dolt.'

'The tomato plants . . . I trust they are well?'

'They are dead. Burned to a frazzle. Withered. Finished.'

Thunderous laughter. Men with dirty great pints in their hands are choking with glee.

'May I inquire into your zinnias?'

'They look as if they have been nursed by a blow lamp.'
'And how are your dwarf dahlias?'
'Wiped out.'
People are crying with laughter. They are sobbing with pure glee.
'Your asters? Your sunflowers? Your marrows? Your cinerarias?'
'Scorched. Doomed. Had it.'
Complete strangers come up to me and shake me by the hand
saying: 'Funniest thing I've ever heard of. You've really made my
day. Thanks awfully old man. You've properly bucked me up.'

CASSANDRA (SIR WILLIAM CONNOR),
Daily Mirror, 14 May 1963

Wilfrid Blunt brought about his own downfall by writing rashly in a newspaper.

The danger the publication of ill-considered enthusiasm may lead to was very forcibly brought home to me when, long ago now, for a year or two I ran the gardening column in the *Sunday Times*. One October I had extolled the beauty of *Tulipa fosterana* (then called *fosteriana*), and recommended, with a journalist's gush, its immediate purchase and planting on a massive scale: 'If you can only afford a dozen, then buy a dozen. If you can afford a hundred, buy a hundred. But if you can afford a thousand, when May comes you will bless me.' I had myself bought, for my cat-run at Eton, half a dozen bulbs, one of which was to forget to put in an appearance. So I was not a little embarrassed when in the following spring the secretary of an Essex ladies' gardening club announced her intention of bringing two coachloads of its members to see my tulips at the height of their glory.

WILFRID BLUNT,
A Gardener's Dozen, 1980

Of course, poor Mr Pooter had no luck at all. He started with mustard and cress and radishes, but nothing came up, and he later had a tiff with Carrie about his annuals.

April 14. Spent the whole of the afternoon in the garden, having this morning picked up at a bookstall for fivepence a capital little book, in good condition, on *Gardening*. I procured and sowed some half-hardy annuals in what I fancy will be a warm, sunny border. I thought of a joke, and called out Carrie. Carrie came out rather testy, I thought. I said: 'I have just discovered I have got a lodging-house.' She replied: 'How do you mean?' I said: '*Look at the boarders.*' Carrie said: 'Is that all that you wanted me for?' I said: 'Any other time you would have laughed at my little pleasantry.' Carrie said: 'Certainly – *at any other time*, but not when I am busy in the house.'

GEORGE AND WEEDON GROSSMITH,
The Diary of a Nobody
(originally published in *Punch*, later in book form in 1892)

The garden is a home for creatures as well as plants, and the most welcome are the birds. Except for the hateful pigeons, which are fat and ugly as well as greedy, I love all my garden birds, which make the place twitter like an aviary in spring. In late autumn, when the flowers look dismal, the bluetits and nuthatches provide a new sort of cheerfulness, and in mid-winter the woodpeckers are brilliant against the snow.

Luckily, gardeners have for centuries enjoyed the company of birds, and although fruit production was formerly far more important than it is today, when so much is imported, have gladly given birds a share of the crops in return for their song.

In William Lawson's time, there were nightingales in the garden.

One chief grace that adorns an Orchard, I cannot let slip: a brood of Nightingales, who with several notes and tunes, with a strong delightsome voice out of a weak body, will bear you company night and day. She loves (and lives in) hots of woods in her heart. She will help you to cleanse your trees of Caterpillars, and all noysome worms and flies. The gentle Robin-red-brest will help her, and in winter in the coldest storms will keep apart. Neither will the silly Wren be behind in Summer, with her distinct whistle, (like a sweet Recorder) to chear your spirits.

The Black-bird and Throstle (for I take it, the Thrush sings not, but devours) sing loudly in a *May* morning, and delights the ear much, and you need not want their company, if you have ripe Cherries or Berries, and would as gladly as the rest do your pleasure: but I had rather want their company than my fruit.

WILLIAM LAWSON,
A New Orchard and Garden, 1618

Joseph Addison, too, to the surprise of his neighbours, was hospitable to birds.

There is another circumstance in which I am very particular, or, as my neighbours call me, very whimsical: as my garden invites into it all the birds of the country, by offering them the conveniency of springs and shades, solitude and shelter, I do not suffer any one to destroy their nests in the spring, or drive them from their usual haunts in fruit-time. I value my garden more for being full of blackbirds than cherries, and very frankly give them fruit for their songs. By this means I have always the musick of the season in its perfection, and am highly delighted to see the jay or the thrush hopping about my walks, and shooting before my eye across the several little glades and alleys that I pass through.

JOSEPH ADDISON,
letter to the *Spectator*, 1712

But Parson Woodforde, a delightful man in other respects, destroyed birds indiscriminately, including those which do no harm.

I shot a Wood-pecker this Morn in my garden.

PARSON WOODFORDE,
Diary, 1788

John Clare observed the birds with the patience and understanding he gave to all country matters and proved them eminently useful. (He was not a good speller, or mathematician for that matter.)

Thurs. 26 May Took up my hyacinth bulbs & laid them in ridges of earth to dry — made a new frame for my Ariculas — found a large white orchis in Oxey Wood of a curious species and very rare I watched a Bluecap or Blue Titmouse feeding her young whose nest was in a wall close to an Orchard she got caterpillars out of the Blossoms of the apple trees and leaves of the plumb — she fetched 120 Caterpillars in half an hour — now supposing she only feeds them 4 times a day a quarter of an hour each time she fetches in no less than 480 Caterpillars & I should think treble that number.

JOHN CLARE,
Journal, 1825

Not all gardeners are so welcoming, however, and a correspondent to a
horticultural magazine in 1832 reported an extraordinary method of keeping
bird pests at bay. I don't know what the R.S.P.C.A. would think of it.

I beg leave to communicate to the Society an easy method of
preserving fruit trees and gardens from the depredation of birds, as
adopted by my friend, Robert Brooke, Esq. . . . He has four or five
Cats, each with a collar, a light chain and swivel, about a yard long
with a large iron ring at the end; as soon as Gooseberries, Currants,
and Raspberries begin to ripen, a small stake is driven into the
ground, or bed, near the trees to be protected, leaving about a yard
and a half of the stake above ground; the ring is slipped over the
head of the stake, and the cat thus tethered in sight of trees, no birds
will approach them. Cherry trees and wall fruit trees are protected
in the same manner as they successively ripen; each cat, by way of
a shed, has one of the largest sized flower pots laid on its side, within
reach of its chain, with a little hay or straw in bad weather, and her
food and water placed near her.

ANONYMOUS,
Transactions of the Horticultural Society, 1832

*Shakespeare sometimes thought of a whole country as a fertile garden, and
mourned its ravaging by civil or foreign war. In* Richard II, *the garden is
a symbol of England; in* Henry V, *the Duke of Burgundy laments the
ruined husbandry of the garden of France.*

[*The Duke of York's garden. The Queen and Ladies hidden. Enter a gardener and two
servants.*]

GARDENER: Go, bind thou up yon dangling apricocks,
Which, like unruly children, make their sire
Stoop with oppression of their prodigal weight:
Give some supportance to the bending twigs.
Go thou, and like an executioner,
Cut off the heads of too fast growing sprays,
That look too lofty in our commonwealth:
All must be even in our government.
You thus employ'd I will go root away
The noisome weeds, that without profit suck
The soil's fertility from wholesome flowers.

FIRST SERVANT: Why should we in the compass of a pale
Keep law and form and due proportion,
Showing, as in a model, our firm estate,
When our sea-walled garden, the whole land,
Is full of weeds, her fairest flowers chok'd up,
Her fruit-trees all unprun'd, her hedges ruin'd,
Her knots disorder'd, and her wholesome herbs
Swarming with caterpillars?

GARDENER: Hold thy peace:
He that hath suffer'd this disorder'd spring
Hath now himself met with the fall of leaf;

The weeds that his broad-spreading leaves did shelter;
That seem'd in eating him to hold him up,
Are pluck'd up root and all by Bolingbroke.

WILLIAM SHAKESPEARE,
Richard II

[After Agincourt. In the French King's Palace at Troyes.]
THE DUKE OF BURGUNDY:

> If I demand before this royal view,
> What rub or what impediment there is,
> Why that the naked, poor, and mangled Peace,
> Dear nurse of arts, plenties, and joyful births,
> Should not in this best garden of the world,
> Our fertile France, put up her lovely visage?
> Alas! she hath from France too long been chas'd,
> And all her husbandry doth lie on heaps,
> Corrupting in its own fertility.
> Her vine, the merry cheerer of the heart,
> Unpruned dies; her hedges even-pleach'd,
> Like prisoners wildly overgrown with hair,
> Put forth disorder'd twigs; her fallow leas
> The darnel, hemlock and rank fumitory
> Doth root upon, while that the coulter rusts
> That should deracinate such savagery;
> The even mead, that erst brought sweetly forth
> The freckled cowslip, burnet, and green clover,
> Wanting the scythe, all uncorrected, rank,
> Conceives by idleness, and nothing teems
> But hateful docks, rough thistle, kecksies, burs,
> Losing both beauty and utility;
> And as our vineyards, fallows, meads, and hedges,
> Defective in their natures, grow to wildness,
> Even so our houses and ourselves and children
> Have lost, or do not learn for want of time,
> The sciences that should become our country.

WILLIAM SHAKESPEARE,
Henry V

Cyril Connolly, too, uses the garden to represent a larger sphere.

It is closing time in the gardens of the West and from now on an artist will be judged by the resonance of his solitude or the quality of his despair.

CYRIL CONNOLLY,
Horizon, December 1949–January 1950

The seventeenth century was the century of delight, and the word is nowhere more frequently and joyously used than in William Lawson's A New Orchard and Garden, *the first classic of the small garden, and the greatest. Lawson was a Yorkshireman and his book is a practical work about north-country gardening, but it is written in the same rich, spontaneous language as King James's Bible.* A New Orchard *was an instant best-seller and ran into at least ten editions in its own century.*

In the last chapter Lawson, his practical message delivered, lets himself go on the delights of an orchard, which 'makes all our senses swim in pleasure', and I wish I could quote it all. The word 'orchard', by the way, includes the whole pleasure garden.

CHAPTER XVII
Ornaments

Methinks hitherto we have but a bare Orchard for fruit, and but half good, so long as it wants those comely Ornaments that should give beauty to all our labours, and make much for the honest delight of the owner and his friends.

Delight the chief end of Orchards.

For it is not to be doubted, but as God hath given man

things profitable, so hath he allowed him honest comfort, delight, and recreation, in all the works of his hands. Nay, all his labours under the Sun without this are troubles and vexations of mind: For what is greedy gain without delight, but moiling, and turmoiling in slavery? But comfortable delight, with content, is the good of every thing, and the pattern of Heaven. A morsel of bread with comfort, is better by much than a fat Ox with unquietness. And who can deny but the principal end of an Orchard, is the honest delight of one wearied with the work of his lawful calling? . . . Of all other delights on earth, they that are taken by Orchards are most excellent, and most agreeing with nature.

This delights all the senses. For whereas every other pleasure commonly fills some one of our senses, and that only with delight; this makes all our senses swim in pleasure and that with infinite variety, joyned with no less commodity . . .

Causes of delight in any Orchard. What can your eye desire to see, your ears to hear, your mouth to take, or your nose to smell, that is not to be had in an Orchard, with abundance of variety? What more delightsome than an infinite variety of sweet smelling flowers, decking with sundry colours, the green mantle of the earth, the universal mother of us all, so by them bespotted, so died, that all the World cannot sample them, and wherein it is more fit to admire the Dyer, than imitate his Workmanship, colouring not only the earth, but decking the air, and sweetning every breath and spirit.

Flowers. The Rose red, Damask, Velvet, and double double Province-Rose, the sweet Musk-Rose double and single, the double and single white-Rose: The fair and sweet-senting Woodbine, double and single, and double double. Purple Cowslips, and double Cowslips, and double double Cowslips, Primrose double and single. The Violet nothing behind the best, for smelling sweetly. A thousand more will provoke your content.

Borders and Squares. And all these by the skill of your Gardiner, so comelily and orderly placed in your borders and squares, and so intermingled, that one looking thereon, cannot but wonder to see, what Nature, corrected by Art, can do.

When you behold in divers corners of your Orchard *Mounts* of stone or wood, curiously wrought within and without, or of earth covered with Fruit-trees, Kentish Cherries, Damsons, Plums, &c. with stairs of precious workmanship; and in some corner (or more) a true Dial or Clock, and some Antick works; and especially silver-sounding Musick, mixt Instruments, and Voices, gracing all the rest: How will you be wrapt with Delight? *Mounts. Whence you may shoot a Buck. Dial. Musick.*

Large Walks, broad and long, close and open, like the *Tempe*-groves in *Thessaly*, raised with gravel and sand, having seats and banks of Camomile; all this delights the mind, and brings health to the body. *Walks. Seats.*

View now with delight the works of your own hands, your Fruit-trees of all sorts, loaden with sweet blossoms, and fruit of all tastes, operations, and colours: your trees standing in comely order, which way soever you look. *Order of trees.*

Your border on every side hanging and dropping with Feberries, Raspberries, Barberries, Currans, and the Roots of your trees powdered with Strawberries, Red, White and Green, what a pleasure is this! Your Gardner can frame your lesser wood to the shape of men armed in the field, ready to give battle; of swift-running Grey-hounds, or of well-sented and true-running Hounds to chase the Deer, or hunt the Hare. This kind of hunting shall not waste your Corn, nor much your Coyn. *Shape of men and beasts.*

Mazes well framed a man's height, may perhaps make your friend wander in gathering of Berries till he cannot recover himself without your help. *Mazes.*

To have occasion to exercise within your Orchard, it shall be a pleasure to have a bowling-Alley, or rather (which is more manly, and more healthful) a pair of Buts, to stretch your Arms. *Bowling-Alley. Buts.*

Rosemary and sweet Eglantine are seemly Ornaments about a Door or Window, and so is Woodbine . . . *Herbs.*

And in mine own opinion, I could highly commend your Orchard, if either through it, or hard by it, there should run River. a pleasant River with silver streams, you might sit in your Mount, and angle a peckled Trout, sleighty Eel, or some other Moats. dainty Fish. Or Moats, whereon you may row with a Boat, and fish with Nets.

Bees. Store of Bees in a warm and dry Bee-house, comely made of Fir-boards, to sing, and sit, and feed upon your flowers and sprouts, make a pleasant noise and sight. For cleanly and innocent Bees, of all other things, love, and become, and thrive in an Orchard . . .

Vine. A Vine overshadowing a seat, is very comely, though her Grapes with us ripen slowly . . .

WILLIAM LAWSON,
A New Orchard and Garden, 1618

The delight of gardening in the seventeenth century was not confined to the rich.

We may without vanity conclude, that a garden of pleasant avenues, walks, fruits, flowers, grots, and other branches springing from it, well composed, is the only compleat and permanent inanimate object of delight the world affords, ever complying with our various and mutable minds, feeding us, and supplying our fancies with daily novels . . .

Such is its pre-excellency, that there is scarce a cottage in most of the southern parts of England, but hath its proportionable garden, so great a delight do most men take in it.

JOHN WORLIDGE,
Systema Horticulturae
or The Art of Gardening, 1667

*By the eighteenth century, delight is less noticeable, and flowers fade into the
background until they are completely banished (along with fruit and
vegetables) by Capability Brown. Now, rational thought takes the place of
green fingers. Pictorial beauty, child of a marriage between nature and art,
is the new objective, and its foremost spokesman is Pope, one of the very few
poets who can make the heroic couplet sparkle.*

> To build, to plant, whatever you intend,
> To tear the Column, or the Arch to bend,
> To swell the Terras, or to sink the Grot;
> In all, let Nature never be forgot . . .
>   Consult the Genius of the Place in all;
> That tells the Waters or to rise or fall,
> Or helps th' ambitious Hill the heav'ns to scale,
> Or scoops in circling theatres the Vale;
> Calls in the Country, catches op'ning glades,
> Joins willing woods, and varies shades from shades;
> Now breaks, or now directs, th' intending Lines,
> Paints as you plant, and as you work, designs.
>   Still follow Sense, of ev'ry Art the Soul,
> Parts answ'ring parts shall slide into a whole,
> Spontaneous beauties all around advance,
> Start ev'n from Difficulty, strike from Chance;
> Nature shall join you; Time shall make it grow
> A Work to wonder at — perhaps a STOW.

ALEXANDER POPE,
An Epistle to Lord Burlington, 1731

Horace Walpole, arbiter of taste in the eighteenth century, also revered the man-made landscape as the garden ideal.

At that moment appeared [William] Kent, painter enough to taste the charms of landscape, bold and opinionative enough to dare and to dictate, and born with a genius to strike out a great system from the twilight of imperfect essays. He leaped the fence, and saw that all nature was a garden. He felt the delicious contrast of hill and valley changing imperceptibly into each other, tasted the beauty of the gentle swell, or concave scoop, and remarked how loose groves crowned an easy eminence with happy ornament . . . The pencil of his imagination bestowed all the arts of landscape on the scenes he handled. The great principles on which he worked were perspective, and light and shade.

HORACE WALPOLE,
On Modern Gardening, 1770

Flowers returned to favour in the nineteenth century, largely through the influence of cottage gardeners. Some, like Miss Mitford of Our Village, were gentry, but others were genuine peasants, like John Clare, who was a highly skilled gardener as well as a collector of wild and old-fashioned plants.

Where rustic taste at leisure trimly weaves
The rose and straggling woodbine to the eaves,
And on the crowded spot that pales enclose
The white and scarlet daisy rears in rows,
Training the trailing peas in bunches neat,
Perfuming evening with a luscious sweet,
And sun-flowers planted for their gilded show,
That scale the window's lattice ere they blow.

                        The timid maid,
Pleased to be praised, and yet of praise afraid,
Seeks the best flowers; not those of wood and fields,
But such as every farmer's garden yields —
Fine cabbage-roses, painted like her face,
The shining pansy, trimm'd with golden lace,
The tall-topped larkheels, feather'd thick with flowers,
The woodbine, climbing o'er the door in bowers,
The London tufts, of many a mottled hue,
The pale pink pea, and monkshood darkly blue,
The white and purple gilliflowers, that stay
Ling'ring, in blossom, summer half away,
The single blood-walls, of a luscious smell,
Old-fashion'd flowers which housewives love so well,
The columbines, stone-blue, or deep night-brown,
Their honeycomb-like blossoms hanging down
Each cottage-garden's fond adopted child,
Though heaths still claim them, where they yet grow wild.

JOHN CLARE,
pieces from two cottage poems, early 1820s

I like this glimpse of a cottage garden in a highly entertaining novel by Mrs Oliphant. Mr Cavendish has got into a terrible mess with his love affairs.

By this time it was getting dark, and it was very pleasant in Grove Street, where most of the good people had just watered their little gardens, and brought out the sweetness of the mignonette. Mr Cavendish was not sentimental, but still the hour was not without its influence; and when he looked at the lights that began to appear in the parlour windows, and breathed in the odours from the little gardens, it is not to be denied that he asked himself for a moment what was the good of going through all this bother and vexation, and whether love in a cottage, with a little garden full of mignonette and a tolerable amount of comfort within, was not, after all, a great deal more reasonable than it looked at first sight.

MRS OLIPHANT
Miss Marjoribanks, 1865

Fact, not fiction: Miss Jekyll, one of the most influential gardeners of all time, loved cottage gardens, used cottage ideas in her garden designing, and restored to cultivation many disappearing cottage flowers.

Some of the most delightful of all gardens are the little strips in front of roadside cottages. They have a simple and tender charm that one may look for in vain in gardens of greater pretension. And the old garden flowers seem to know that there they are seen at their best; for where else can one see such Wallflowers, or Double Daisies, or White Rose bushes; such clustering masses of perennial Peas, or such well-kept flowery edgings of Pink, or Thrift, or London Pride?

GERTRUDE JEKYLL,
Wood and Garden, 1899

The affectations of gardeners have inspired some pearls of wit. Women are usually the butt. E. F. Benson's Lucia books are among the funniest of light novels, full of ludicrous incidents and pretentious people. The heroine, Mrs Lucas, known as Lucia, is the uncrowned queen of society in her village of Riseholme, but when she moves house from Riseholme to the small town of Tilling she comes up against a rival, the fiendish Miss Mapp. The snobberies, affectations and jealousies of the two ladies at Tilling are mercilessly exposed by E. F. Benson's waspish pen, and the competitive spirit of Lucia and Miss Mapp reaches sublime heights in the garden.

Benson himself lived in the town on which Tilling is based, Rye, in Sussex, inhabiting the house formerly lived in by Henry James. When asked who was the original of Miss Mapp, he said it was himself.

'My little plot,' said Miss Mapp. 'Very modest, as you see, three-quarters of an acre at the most, but well screened. My flower-beds: sweet roses, tortoise-shell butterflies. Rather a nice clematis. My Little Eden I call it, so small, but so well beloved.'

'Enchanting!' said Lucia, looking round the garden before mounting the steps up to the garden-room door. There was a very green and well-kept lawn, set in bright flower-beds. A trellis at one end separated it from a kitchen-garden beyond, and round the rest ran high brick walls, over which peered the roofs of other houses. In one of these walls was cut a curved archway with a della Robbia head above it.

'Shall we just pop across the lawn,' said Miss Mapp, pointing to this, 'and peep in there while Withers brings our tea? Just to stretch the – the limbs, Mrs Lucas, after your long drive. There's a wee little plot beyond there which is quite a pet of mine. And here's sweet Puss-Cat come to welcome my friends. Lamb! Love-bird!'

Love-bird's welcome was to dab rather crossly at the caressing hand which its mistress extended, and to trot away to ambush itself beneath some fine hollyhocks where it regarded them with singular disfavour

'My little secret garden,' continued Miss Mapp as they came to the archway. 'When I am in here and shut the door, I mustn't be disturbed for anything less than a telegram. A rule of the house: I am very strict about it. The tower of the church keeping watch, as I always say, over my little nook, and taking care of me. Otherwise not overlooked at all. A little paved walk round it, you see, flower-beds, a pocket-handkerchief of a lawn, and in the middle a pillar with a bust of good Queen Anne. Picked it up in a shop here for a song. One of my lucky days.'

'Oh Georgie, isn't it too sweet?' cried Lucia. 'Un giardino segreto. Molto bello!'

E. F. BENSON,
Mapp and Lucia, 1931

If E. F. Benson was a wasp, Beverley Nichols was a hornet.

She arrived with a charming friend of mine, on to whom she had attached herself like a pale but determined leech. She stayed for a week. Both my friend and I were driven to the verge of hysteria by her posing and her terrible determination to 'appreciate' things, but what could one do? One could not turn her out. I dropped hints, on more than one occasion, that other guests were expected, but she only opened her eyes innocently and said 'Who?' And, as I could never think of anybody, on the spur of the moment, but the Aga Khan (for whom she appeared to entertain a peculiar passion), this ruse cannot be described as very successful.

'Oh . . . oh . . . but it's Honeymoon Cottage! . . .' she cried, clasping her hands, and opening her mouth very wide, as she first stepped into my garden.

There is no reply to this sort of remark, so I did a sort of gurgle.

'No . . . no . . .' she breathed, putting one hand over her eyes, 'don't . . . don't say anything. Listen.'

I listened. All I could hear were some pigs making slightly obscene noises in a neighbouring farm. I looked at her inquiringly. Had she a pig complex, or something?

'The peace of it,' she hissed, 'the peace!'

She drew a long drawn sigh, and opened her eyes again. Her eyelids fluttered madly for a moment. Then, like a brave little thing, she forced a smile to her lips, drew my arm through hers, and murmured, 'Show me . . . show me . . . *everything*.'

Checking the indelicate thought that she was making 'a certain suggestion' to me (as the Sunday newspapers would say), I showed her round the garden. It was agony. For she had the curious illusion, entertained by so many affected women, that her ignorance was charming. She would poke her parasol into a clump of lupins, to their infinite peril, and say 'lovely . . . *lovely* canterbury bells!' I began by correcting her, but I soon desisted, because I found that she said these things merely in order to be corrected, so that she might mince about and giggle and say 'What a little town mouse I am!' (she said this quite often, and she pronounced it 'toon moose').

So finally, when she pushed her rather large and thickly powdered nose into a bush of honeysuckle, murmured 'divine jasmine', and looked at me over her shoulder for the expected correction, I did not play up. I said 'Yes, isn't it?' She looked quite hurt . . . like a child deprived of its toy.

After she had been with us for two days, her affectations became almost intolerable. She was always posing in ultra-old-world positions all over the garden. While one was squashing beetles or pulling up weeds she would drape herself against a tree or a bush, fondly imagining that she thereby enhanced its beauty . . .

I never knew a woman who took so many impedimenta into a garden. She had, for example, a huge hat with ribbons, which she swung girlishly over one arm . . . She also had a huge shallow basket, of beige-coloured straw with a pale blue ribbon threaded round the sides. It was a silly, vilely unpractical basket. Everything fell out of it.

BEVERLEY NICHOLS,
Down the Garden Path, 1932

Two powerful minds of the seventeenth century conceived an ideal garden. One charms me, the other repels me. Sir Francis Bacon's heath, approached through an elaborate Elizabethan garden, is an exquisite blend of wildness with design. It is a gardener's garden.

For gardens (speaking of those which are indeed prince-like, as we have done of buildings), the contents ought not well to be under thirty acres of ground, and to be divided into three parts: a green in the entrance; a heath or desert in the going forth; and the main garden in the midst; besides alleys on both sides. And I like well that four acres of ground be assigned to the green; six to the heath; four and four to either side; and twelve to the main garden . . .

For the heath, which was the third part of our plot, I wish it to be framed, as much as may be, to a natural wildness. Trees I would have none in it; but some thickets, made only of sweet-briar and honeysuckle, and some wild vine amongst; and the ground set with violets, strawberries, and primroses. For these are sweet, and prosper in the shade. And these to be in the heath, here and there, not in any order. I like also little heaps, in the nature of mole-hills (such as are in wild heaths), to be set, some with wild thyme; some with pinks; some with germander, that gives a good flower to the eye; some with periwinkle; some with violets; some with strawberries; some with cowslips; some with daisies; some with red roses; some with bear's-foot; and the like low flowers, being withal sweet and sightly. Part of which heaps to be with standards of little bushes pricked upon their top, and part without. The standards to be roses; juniper; holly; berberries (but here and there, because of the smell of their blossom); red currans; gooseberries; rosemary; bays; sweet-briar, and such like. But these standards to be kept with cutting, that they grow not out of course.

SIR FRANCIS BACON,
Essay of Gardens, 1625

Adam and Eve's bower in Paradise Lost, *on the other hand, is too luxuriant for my taste, distinctly overplanted.*

Thus talking hand in hand alone they pass'd
On to their blissful bower; it was a place
Chosen by the sov'reign planter, when he fram'd
All things to man's delightful use: the roof
Of thickest covert was inwoven shade,
Laurel and myrtle, and what higher grew
Of firm and fragrant leaf; on either side
Acanthus and each odorous bushy shrub
Fenc'd up the verdant wall, each beauteous flow'r,
Iris all hues, roses, and jessamin
Rear'd high their flourish'd heads between, and wrought
Mosaic; under foot the violet,
Crocus, and hyacinth with rich inlay
Broider'd the ground, more colour'd than with stone
Of costliest emblem: other creature here,
Beast, bird, insect, or worm, durst enter none;
Such was their awe of man. In shadier bower
More sacred and sequester'd, though but feign'd,
Pan or Sylvanus never slept; nor nymph,
Nor Faunus haunted. Here in close recess
With flowers, garlands, and sweet-smelling herbs,
Espoused Eve deck'd first her nuptial bed . . .

JOHN MILTON,
Paradise Lost, Book IV

Milton would have been shocked at Charles Lamb's irreverence.

A garden was the primitive prison, till man, with Promethean felicity and boldness, luckily sinned himself out of it.

CHARLES LAMB,
letter to Wordsworth, 1830

The case for and against the landscape garden and the picturesque was
argued so ferociously in print through the eighteenth century by Pope,
Walpole, those two old bores, Richard Payne Knight and Sir Uvedale
Price, and countless others, that one might suppose that the country gentlemen
of England were engaged in a civil war. Luckily, there were satiric pens to
correct this absurd impression. Peacock takes off the 'improvers' to a T in
Headlong Hall. *Mr Milestone is based on Humphry Repton, who supplied*
each prospective client with a Red Book showing what his property looked
like – and what it could look like with 'the finger of taste'.

CHAPTER IV
The Grounds

'I perceive,' said Mr Milestone, after they had walked a few paces,
'these grounds have never been touched by the finger of taste.'

'The place is quite a wilderness,' said Squire Headlong: 'for during
the latter part of my father's life, while I was *finishing* my *education*,
he troubled himself about nothing but the cellar, and suffered every
thing else to go to rack and ruin. A mere wilderness, as you see, even
now in December; but in summer a complete nursery of briers, a
forest of thistles, a plantation of nettles, without any live stock but
goats, that have eaten up all the bark of the trees. Here you see is the
pedestal of a statue, with only half a leg and four toes remaining:
there were many here once. When I was a boy, I used to sit every day
on the shoulders of Hercules: what became of *him* I have never been
able to ascertain. Neptune has been lying these seven years in the
dust-hole; Atlas had his head knocked off to fit him for propping a
shed, and only the day before yesterday we fished Bacchus out of the
horse-pond.'

'My dear sir,' said Mr Milestone, 'accord me your permission to
wave the wand of enchantment over your grounds. The rocks shall
be blown up, the trees shall be cut down, the wilderness and all its
goats shall vanish like mist. Pagodas and Chinese bridges, gravel
walks and shrubberies, bowling-greens, canals, and clumps of larch,
shall rise upon its ruins. One age, sir, has brought to light the
treasures of ancient learning; a second has penetrated into the depths

of metaphysics; a third has brought to perfection the science of astronomy; but it was reserved for the exclusive genius of the present times, to invent the noble art of picturesque gardening, which has given, as it were, a new tint to the complexion of nature, and a new outline to the physiognomy of the universe!'

'Give me leave,' said Sir Patrick O'Prism, 'to take an exception to that same. Your system of levelling, and trimming, and clipping, and docking, and clumping, and polishing, and cropping, and shaving, destroys all the beautiful intricacies of natural luxuriance, and all the graduated harmonies of light and shade, melting into one another, as you see them on that rock over yonder. I never saw one of your improved places, as you call them, and which are nothing but big bowling-greens, like sheets of green paper, with a parcel of round clumps scattered over them, like so many spots of ink, flicked at random out of a pen, and a solitary animal here and there looking as if it were lost, that I did not think it was for all the world like Hounslow Heath, thinly sprinkled over with bushes and highway-men.'

'Sir,' said Mr Milestone, 'you will have the goodness to make a distinction between the picturesque and the beautiful.'

'Will I?' said Sir Patrick, 'och! but I won't. For what is beautiful? That which pleases the eye. And what pleases the eye? Tints variously broken and blended. Now, tints variously broken and blended constitute the picturesque.'

'Allow me,' said Mr Gall. 'I distinguish the picturesque and the beautiful, and I add to them, in the laying out of grounds, a third and distinct character, which I call *unexpectedness*.'

'Pray, sir,' said Mr Milestone, 'by what name do you distinguish this character, when a person walks round the grounds for the second time?'

Mr Gall bit his lips, and inwardly vowed to revenge himself on Milestone, by cutting up his next publication.

THOMAS LOVE PEACOCK,
Headlong Hall, 1816

Jane Austen was another novelist who poked fun at Repton.

She [Fanny] must try to find amusement in what was passing at the upper end of the table, and in observing Mr Rushworth, who was now making his appearance at Mansfield, for the first time since the Crawfords' arrival. He had been visiting a friend in a neighbouring county, and that friend having recently had his grounds laid out by an improver, Mr Rushworth was returned with his head full of the subject, and very eager to be improving his own place in the same way; and though not saying much to the purpose, could talk of nothing else . . .

'I wish you could see Compton,' said he, 'it is the most complete thing! I never saw a place so altered in my life. I told Smith I did not know where I was. The approach *now* is one of the finest things in the country. You see the house in the most surprising manner. I declare when I got back to Sotherton yesterday, it looked like a prison – quite a dismal old prison.'

'Oh! for shame!' cried Mrs Norris. 'A prison, indeed! Sotherton Court is the noblest old place in the world.'

'It wants improvement, ma'am, beyond any thing. I never saw a place that wanted so much improvement in my life; and it is so forlorn, that I do not know what can be done with it.'

'No wonder that Mr Rushworth should think so at present,' said Mrs Grant to Mrs Norris, with a smile; 'but depend upon it, Sotherton will have *every* improvement in time which his heart can desire.'

'I must try to do something with it,' said Mr Rushworth, 'but I do not know what. I hope I shall have some good friend to help me.'

'Your best friend upon such an occasion,' said Miss Bertram, calmly, 'would be Mr Repton, I imagine.'

'That is what I was thinking of. As he has done so well by Smith, I think I had better have him at once. His terms are five guineas a day.'

JANE AUSTEN,
Mansfield Park, 1814

In spite of Peacock's and Miss Austen's jibes, Repton was a highly popular man. He started life in the textile trade, but switched with cheerful resilience to landscape gardening, and was an instant success.

Now at the age of 36 years – I commence a new career – and after a temporary rest – and half seclusion from the world; I boldly venture forth once more, and with renewed energy and hope push off my little bark into a sea unknown.

HUMPHRY REPTON,
Memoir, 1788

*Insects and pests often take up as much gardening time as the creative jobs,
like planting. Some gardeners are obsessed with earwigs.*

> Sylphs! on each oak-bed wound the wormy galls,
> With pygmy spears, or crush the venom'd balls;
> Fright the green locust from his foamy bed,
> Unweave the caterpillar's gluey thread;
> Chase the fierce earwig, scare the bloated toad,
> Arrest the snail upon his slimy road.

ERASMUS DARWIN,
The Economy of Vegetation, 1791

*This good lady, writing to a gardening magazine in 1982, had her own
way of dealing with the pests.*

Our earwig traps are not at all unsightly. We crush sheets of
newspaper into fairly tight balls, hide them among the dahlia
foliage, and overnight the earwigs crawl into the screwed up paper.

Then, in the morning after breakfast, we go out into the garden,
call to the blackbird, 'Earwigs, Blackie' and he flies down and
quickly devours the earwigs that scurry out as we shake the ball.

ANONYMOUS

Some gardeners have found the pursuit of pests positively stimulating. André Gide was a superb gardener, with a house at Cuverville, in Normandy. He plunged with enthusiasm into even the humblest tasks.

All morning in the garden. I couldn't get myself to go in and write. I come to lunch intoxicated and Em. says that I 'look like a madman'. What have I done to look that way? Merely hunted insects on my rosebushes.

ANDRÉ GIDE,
Journal, year 1905

But there are good insects, too, like ladybirds, and some are even gardeners themselves. Anthony Huxley tells us that certain ants prepare soil and grow fungi in it for food.

Ants also cultivate plants for food. These are the leaf-cutting ants of tropical America, which can defoliate large trees overnight. The leaf fragments, up to 2 cm across, are brought into special chambers in the nests: one observer described how the ants marched in 'like Sunday-school children carrying banners' . . . In the chambers the leaf fragments are chewed up and, with other vegetable debris and ant excrement, a hot-bed is created upon which a special fungus grows, in principle exactly like a modern mushroom grower's beds. The worker ants actively tend these fungi, weeding out any alien growths that may appear, and transplant the fungi to new chambers as these are prepared. Something in the ants' saliva inhibits the growth of unwanted fungi and may also promote the wanted fungus's growth. This fungus, which forms the major food of these ants, is a small subterranean species which has never been seen outside the ants' nests, although this may well be simply because of the problem of knowing where to look. Neither is it known whether the fungus lives naturally in the soil and was originally deliberately brought in by the ants, or grew in their nests by accident and was then cultivated.

ANTHONY HUXLEY,
Plant and Planet, 1974

Slugs are a pest with few friends. I suppose there are molluscologists who are slug-lovers, but I have never met a gardener who could endure them. Vita Sackville-West felt a murderess when she poisoned them, but she did it all the same. As a child I was paid sixpence for a 2-lb jam-jar of salt water filled with dead slugs, which I picked up between two sticks. Mr Bowles had his own method.

I am very fond of the Spring-flowering colchicums, but unfortunately slugs are also, and those greedy gasteropods and I have a race for who can see the flower-buds first. If I win I go out after dark with an acetylene lamp and a hatpin and spear the little army of slugs making for a tea-party at the sign of the Colchicum.

E. A. BOWLES,
My Garden in Spring, 1914

*However, snails have had their admirers. Lord Emsworth enjoyed pursuing
them, presumably as a treat for Empress of Blandings, his prize pig.*

[Lord Emsworth] was humming as he approached the terrace. He
had his programme all mapped out. For perhaps an hour, till the day
had cooled off a little, he would read a Pig book in the library. After
that he would go and take a sniff at a rose or two and possibly do a
bit of snailing. These mild pleasures were all his simple soul
demanded. He wanted nothing more.

P. G. WODEHOUSE,
Lord Emsworth and Others, 1937

Of all the forms of entertaining, a garden party is the most hazardous. Quite apart from the weather, there are grave social risks — guests, unable to mingle, may cluster in static, isolated groups, trying in vain to look animated. E. M. Forster's garden party in India is an exquisitely complex failure.

The Collector kept his word. Next day he issued invitation cards to numerous Indian gentlemen in the neighbourhood, stating that he would be at home in the garden of the club between the hours of five and seven on the following Tuesday, also that Mrs Turton would be glad to receive any ladies of their families who were out of purdah. His action caused much excitement and was discussed in several worlds.

'It is owing to orders from the L. G.,' was Mahmoud Ali's explanation. 'Turton would never do this unless compelled. Those high officials are different — they sympathize, the Viceroy sympathizes, they would have us treated properly. But they come too seldom and live too far away. Meanwhile—'

'It is easy to sympathize at a distance,' said an old gentleman with a beard. 'I value more the kind word that is spoken close to my ear. Mr Turton has spoken it, from whatever cause. He speaks, we hear. I do not see why we need discuss it further.' Quotations followed from the Koran . . .

The Bridge Party was not a success — at least it was not what Mrs Moore and Miss Quested were accustomed to consider a successful party. They arrived early, since it was given in their honour, but most of the Indian guests had arrived even earlier, and stood massed at the farther side of the tennis lawns, doing nothing.

'It is only just five,' said Mrs Turton. 'My husband will be up from his office in a moment and start the thing. I have no idea what we have to do' . . . [Mr Turton arrives.]

'To work, Mary, to work,' cried the Collector, touching his wife on the shoulder with a switch.

Mrs Turton got up awkwardly. 'What do you want me to do? Oh, those purdah women! I never thought any would come. Oh dear!'

A little group of Indian ladies had been gathering in a third quarter of the grounds, near a rustic summer-house in which the more timid of them had already taken refuge. The rest stood with their backs to the company and their faces pressed into a bank of shrubs. At a little distance stood their male relatives, watching the venture. The sight was significant: an island bared by the turning tide, and bound to grow.

'I consider they ought to come over to me.'

'Come along, Mary, get it over.'

'I refuse to shake hands with any of the men, unless it has to be the Nawab Badahur.'

'Whom have we so far?' He glanced along the line. 'H'm! H'm! much as one expected. We know why he's here, I think – over that contract, and he wants to get the right side of me for Mohurram, and he's the astrologer who wants to dodge the municipal building regulations, and he's that Parsi, and he's – Hullo! there he goes – smash into our hollyhocks. Pulled the left rein when he meant the right. As usual.'

'They ought never to have been allowed to drive in: it's so bad for them,' said Mrs Turton . . .

Advancing, she shook hands with the group and said a few words of welcome in Urdu. She had learnt the lingo, but only to speak to her servants, so she knew none of the politer forms and of the verbs only the imperative mood.

E. M. FORSTER,
A Passage to India, 1924

Osbert Sitwell describes a garden party of quite a different order, given by a prince in Peking in 1934.

The advance of the year was so rapid, you could almost hear the branches of apple and quince and wistaria creaking with the life within them, almost see the sticky buds first appear, and then unfold and open into their spice-breathing cups and tongues and turrets. And, since the object of this party was to see the crab-apple trees in bloom, no afternoon could have been more fitted, more consecrated by Nature herself, to this purpose. It might have been fashioned solely for men to savour the scent and essence of such trees in flower, and the gay, sheepskin clouds, flecking the blue dome of the sky, were translucent as the clustered petals themselves . . .

The gardens seemed immense, as we got out of our rickshas and began to walk. Inside the boundaries of their walls, crowned with yellow tiles, were groves of old cypresses, the frond-like arrangements of their leaves lying upon the air as though they were layers of blue-green smoke, there were eighteenth-century water gardens, now dry but full of wild flowers, and there were the sunk gardens wherein flourished, with gnarled, rough trunks, the crooked and ancient fruit trees which constituted the chief pride of their owner . . .

Perhaps they could scarcely be termed orchards, because the trees, being grown for their blossom rather than their fruit, were irregularly disposed, and were fewer to the given area than is our custom. Bent, contorted with age as the old men who were now on their way to inspect them, they must have been planted some two centuries before. Each of them might have been shaped by the green fingers of a Chinese God of Growth, each was as exquisitely placed upon the green turf as any figure upon a scroll by the hand of a great artist. Perfect in their balance and grotesque posture, some inclined, at the precise angle best calculated to display their unexpected and singular grace, while one tree, even, lay on its side and blossomed on the ground.

Slowly, painfully, the old men hobbled along the crooked, paved paths that zigzagged to these trees. When they reached them, they were conducted up small flights of stone steps, so fashioned that, saving where the steps showed, they seemed natural rocks that had cropped up through the turf or had fallen from the sky. These flights, their tops level with the tops of the trees, are thus placed near apple and pear and peach and quince and cherry, so that the connoisseur can obtain a perfect view of the blossom. Even to a newcomer, inexpert in the flowery lore of the Chinese, from each different plane, the particular view of the tree for which the step had been constructed offered a revelation of a new world; of the same kind as when first you fly in an aircraft above the clouds, and look down upon their fleecy humps, white and golden – except that clouds disperse, are opaque, and do not favour an ordered development.

To the Chinese amateurs of the garden, however, these steps offer even more than to someone, like myself, who was fresh to them. In consequence, the old gentlemen persevered – for it was difficult for them to ascend such crags . . .

Once there, they would remain for a full hour, matching in their minds the complexion and fragrance of the blossom of previous years with that before them. Then, after the general examination of the crop, came the more intimate tallying of one branch, one flower, one bud, with another, and finally it was necessary again to consider the entire grouping and design. But the bees, inordinately busy and managing, behaving as though they were old women in a market, got in the way, and even the less industrious butterflies obscured the view with their gaudily decorated sails or dragged down a petal too heavily when suddenly they perched upon it . . . Critical appreciation of this high order could not be hurried.

OSBERT SITWELL,
Sing High! Sing Low!, 1944

Biblical scholars have suggested many diverse interpretations of the Song of Solomon, *which is unlike, in language and thought, almost everything else in the Old Testament. Some see it as an allegory, with Christ the bridegroom and the Church the bride. Others see it as a drama with three* dramatis personae: *King Solomon, a shepherd, and the Shulamite beauty. Or it is 'conjugal prattle' between Solomon and the daughter of Pharaoh whom he married. Or it is a sequence of Syrian wedding songs. And so on. Passages which do not fit into each theory are sometimes conveniently dismissed as glosses or interpolations.*

To a non-scholar like myself it is lovely erotic poetry, the allusions to a garden celebrating the joy of consummated love.

A garden inclosed is my sister, my spouse; a spring shut up, a fountain sealed.

Thy plants are an orchard of pomegranates, with pleasant fruits; camphire, with spikenard,

Spikenard and saffron; calamus and cinnamon, with all trees of frankincense; myrrh and aloes, with all the chief spices:

A fountain of gardens, a well of living waters, and streams from Lebanon.

Awake, O north wind; and come, thou south; blow upon my garden, that the spices thereof may flow out. Let my beloved come into his garden, and eat his pleasant fruits.

I am come into my garden, my sister, my spouse: I have gathered my myrrh with my spice; I have eaten my honeycomb with my honey; I have drunk my wine with my milk: eat, O friends; drink, yea, drink abundantly, O beloved.

Song of Solomon, 4, XII — 5, I

My beloved is gone down into his garden, to the beds of spices, to feed in the gardens and to gather lilies.

I am my beloved's, and my beloved is mine: he feedeth among the lilies.

Song of Solomon, 6, 11, 111

What makes a real gardener? Beverley Nichols says it is ownership, and, thinking of the shortcomings of jobbing gardeners, it's hard to disagree.

You like walking out on to a terrace and looking up at a wall that is covered with the pale, tipsy plumes of wisteria . . . to walk under arches of orange blossom, thinking the prettiest thoughts . . . and you may even stoop down to pick a bunch of pansies, if they match your frock. You like these things, yes.

But you do not like grovelling on the earth in search of a peculiarly nauseating slug that has been eating those pansies. You do not like putting a trowel under the slug, hoping that it will not suddenly burst or produce fearful slime, and tipping the slug with gratified horror into a basket. You do not like bending down for hours to pull up hateful little weeds that break off above the root . . . (not groundsel, because groundsel is a lovely weed to pull up) . . . but small docks and wretched things like that. You do not like these things, for one reason and only one reason . . . because you do not *own* the garden.

All gardeners will know what I mean. Ownership makes all the difference in the world. I suppose it is like the difference between one's own baby and somebody else's. If it is your own baby you probably quite enjoy wiping its nose. If it is somebody else's you

would have to use a long pole with a handkerchief on the end . . .
at least I should.

BEVERLEY NICHOLS,
Down the Garden Path, 1932

Karel Čapek, a Czech whose book is a classic of gardening wit and understanding, published in English in 1931, says the true gardener's first love is the soil.

I find that the real gardener is not a man who cultivates flowers; he is a man who cultivates the soil . . . If he came into the Garden of Eden he would sniff excitedly and say: 'Good Lord, what humus!' I think that he would forget to eat the fruit of the tree of knowledge of good and evil; he would rather look round to see how he could manage to take away from the Lord some barrow-loads of the paradisaic soil. Or he would discover that the tree of knowledge of good and evil has not round it a nice dishlike bed, and he would begin to mess about with the soil, innocent of what is hanging over his head. 'Where are you, Adam?' the Lord would say. 'In a moment,' the gardener would shout over his shoulder; 'I am busy now.' And he would go on making his little bed.

KAREL ČAPEK,
The Gardener's Year, 1931

That fine plantswoman, Beth Chatto, agrees with Čapek about the soil.

Soil is our most valuable commodity . . . Oil and precious elements we could do without, but we were born originally out of the soil and must respect it. As a child I loved the feel and smell of soil and no doubt exasperated my mother by being frequently covered with it.

BETH CHATTO,
The Damp Garden, 1982

In saying that she loved the soil as a child, Beth Chatto touched on something important. Memories of a garden loved in childhood often stir garden longings in later life. I am sure that Stevenson's small boy in the cherry tree became a gardener when he grew up.

Stevenson's verses for children were much loved in my family when I was young. He had a genius for raising vivid little pictures in the mind: a sick child playing with his toys in bed, children playing soldiers, children watching for Leerie, the lamp-lighter (a favourite poem with us, for we were lucky enough to have a gas-lamp in the street outside our door), or a child climbing trees in the garden.

FOREIGN LANDS

Up into the cherry tree
Who should climb but little me?
I held the trunk with both my hands
And looked abroad on foreign lands.

I saw the next door garden lie,
Adorned with flowers before my eye,
And many pleasant places more
That I had never seen before.

ROBERT LOUIS STEVENSON,
A Child's Garden of Verses, 1885

Another characteristic of the true gardener is a love of rain. In 1799
William and Dorothy Wordsworth moved from Somerset to Grasmere in
Westmorland, and there, through 1800 and again in 1802, Dorothy kept
a journal which shows that the Wordsworths' intense joy in nature was
almost equalled by their love of the garden which they made at Dove Cottage.
At that time the Lake District teemed with wild flowers, and they
transplanted many to the garden and orchard.

Friday 28th May. I was much better than yesterday, though poorly.
William tired himself with hammering at a passage. I was out of
spirits. After dinner he was better and I greatly better. We sate in
the orchard. The sky cloudy the air sweet and cool. The young
Bullfinches in their party coloured Raiment bustle about among the
Blossoms and poize themselves like Wire-dancers or tumblers,
shaking the twigs and dashing off the Blossoms. There is yet one
primrose in the orchard. The stitchwort is fading. The wild
columbines are coming into beauty. The vetches are in abundance,
Blossoming and seeding. That pretty little waxy-looking Dial-like
yellow flower [pimpernel], the speedwell, and some others whose
names I do not yet know. The wild columbines are coming into
beauty – some of the gowans fading. In the garden we have lilies and
many other flowers. The scarlet Beans are up in crowds. It is now
between 8 and nine o'clock. It has rained sweetly for two hours and
a half – the air is very mild. The heckberry are dropping off fast,
almost gone – barberries are in beauty – snowballs coming forward
– May roses blossoming.

Journals of Dorothy Wordsworth, 1798–1802

Writers of the seventeenth and eighteenth centuries enjoyed translating Latin poets into English, especially Horace. Matthew Prior turned the following verse.

Great Mother, let me once be able
To have a garden, house and stable;
That I may read, and ride, and plant,
Superior to desire, or want;
And as health fails, and years increase,
Sit down, and think, and die in peace.

MATTHEW PRIOR

The original epode is:

Beatus ille, qui procus negotiis,
Ut prisca gens mortalium,
Paterna rura bubus exercet suis,
Solutus omni faenore.

Somehow, Swift's verse is much more moving.

I often wish'd that I had clear
For life, six hundred pounds a year,
A handsome house to lodge a friend,
A river at my garden's end,
A terrace walk, and half a rood
Of land, set out to plant a wood.

JONATHAN SWIFT,
Imitation of Horace

His inspiration was this Horace satire:

Hoc erat in votis: modus agri non ita magnus,
Hortus ubi et tecto vicinus iugis aquae fons
Et paulum silvae super his foret.

[II. vi. I]

Pope is said to have written this version of the beatus ille *theme at the age of twelve.*

Happy the man whose wish and care
A few paternal acres bound,
Content to breathe his native air,
       In his own ground.

ALEXANDER POPE,
Ode on Solitude

Vita Sackville-West and her husband, Harold Nicolson, created the lovely garden at Sissinghurst Castle, Kent, out of a derelict estate which they refashioned with genius, beginning their lifelong task in 1930. Both, particularly Vita, who was one of the most prolific gardening writers of this century, wrote much about the garden, Vita always in romantic terms. This poem was dedicated to her beloved friend, Virginia Woolf.

A tired swimmer in the waves of time
    I threw my hands up: let the surface close:
Sink down through centuries to another clime,
And buried find the castle and the rose.
    Buried in time and sleep,
    So drowsy, overgrown,
That here the moss is green upon the stone
    And lichen stains the keep.

© Nigel Nicolson

V. SACKVILLE-WEST,
Sissinghurst Castle, 1931

Harold Nicolson was more detached, even to the point of debunking Vita's paradise. He later came to love Sissinghurst as dearly as did his wife, but their first night spent in the castle was not propitious. It was a dank night in autumn, and Harold had had to slosh through the mud carrying groceries, to light a fire with wet wood, and to fill a jug of water from a disused garden pump. At last, having kindled the fire with Vita's best new garden labels, they sat down to dinner.

And then we dined. I am not an exacting man, but there are four things which I hate. One is soup from tablets; another is sardines; a third is tongue; and the fourth is cheese in wedges. All these four things had been selected by Edith [Vita] for my evening meal . . .

'What I like,' said Edith, on re-entering the living room, 'is the mellow light of candles. So soft it is.' It was so soft, indeed, that I was unable to read and at 9.20 p.m. I said I would go to bed. I was very wet and very cold.

© Nigel Nicolson

HAROLD NICOLSON,
B.B.C. broadcast, 1930

Dickens was another realist. The scene is Dingley Dell, the characters the amorous Mr Tupman and the maiden aunt.

There was a bower at the further end, with honeysuckle, jessamine, and creeping plants – one of those sweet retreats which humane men erect for the accommodation of spiders.

CHARLES DICKENS,
The Pickwick Papers, 1836–7

Another gardener who stared the truth in the face — no false promises here — was John Scott, a Quaker poet and a friend of Dr Johnson.

Proceed, my Friend, pursue thy healthful toil,
Dispose thy ground, and meliorate thy soil;
Range thy young plants in walks, or clumps, or bow'rs,
Diffuse o'er sunny banks thy fragrant flow'rs;
And, while the new creation round thee springs,
Enjoy uncheck'd the guiltless bliss it brings:
But hope no more. Though Fancy forward stray
These scenes of distant pleasure to survey,
To expatiate fondly o'er the future grove,
The happy haunt of Friendship and of Love;
Know, each fair image form'd within thy mind,
Far wide of truth thy sickening sight shall find.

JOHN SCOTT
To a Friend, Planting

Whoever else has green fingers, it is not usually the jobbing gardener. For centuries, owners have complained about hired men murdering their best plants, hacking the shrubs to pieces or, ignoring labels, throwing precious treasures on the bonfire along with the weeds. Sometimes they burn the rare plants with such gusto that one wonders if they knew their value all the time. The pig-headed jobbing gardener is not an exclusively modern pest. John Parkinson had something to say about him in 1629.

Our English gardeners are all or most of them utterly ignorant in the ordering of these outlandish [foreign] flowers, as not being trained up to know them . . . And I do wish all gentlemen and gentlewomen, whom it may concern for their own good, to be as careful whom they trust with the planting and replanting of these fine flowers, as they would be with so many jewels; for the roots of many of them being small, and of great value, may be soon conveyed away, and a cleanly tale fair told, that such a root is rotten, or perished in the ground if none can be seen where it should be, or else that flower has changed his colour, when it hath been taken away, or a counterfeit one hath been put in the place thereof; and thus many have been deceived of their daintiest flowers, without remedy or true knowledge of the defect.

JOHN PARKINSON,
Paradisi in Sole, Paradisus Terrestris, 1629

Dr (now Sir) Roy Strong, when making his first garden, in Herefordshire, decided against employing a grouchy old gardener. He felt that anyone making a garden today must think in new terms.

I am thinking all the time of the garden twenty years hence, when all the circumstances will be different. Take the question of labour. It's short-sighted to try for a gardener. There are only a few old-fashioned private gardeners left, whom everyone squabbles over, and in a few years there will be none. I don't want one. I don't want a little old man nestling in the cottage grumbling all the time. For the likes of us, the intellectual poor, all that feudal bit is finished. And I don't want an Old Age Pensioner lacerating the shrubs with a billhook. They ruin everything. I want to work with young people. I wouldn't mind an off-beat youth with long hair if I could get one.

DR ROY STRONG,
in an interview with Anne Scott-James,
Harpers & Queen, February 1974

In the United States, Eleanor Perényi, making a garden in Connecticut,
found the jobbing gardener equally unsatisfactory. Only one out of a long
procession of hired helpers grew to love the garden, and even he never learned
the name of a single plant.

Well-trained gardeners who like their work must live in America,
but not around here and not in my price range. When I look back
on the long procession of incompetents, dumbbells and eccentrics,
young and old, foreign and domestic, who have worked for me, I
wonder how I and the garden have survived their ministrations. I
recall, for example, Mr R., a well-known figure in town because in
spite of his shabby get-up he is said to be very rich, with large
plantations in Brazil – or it may be the Cape Verde Islands. You see
him moving at a rapid hobble along the street, on his way to some
garden or other, usually belonging to a newcomer because we old-
timers know that he brings death and destruction with him. Those
he has worked for discuss him with tears in their eyes. The summer
he gardened for me he killed two cherry trees, uprooted a plantation
of Dutch iris and imparted crooked lines to the perennial beds from
which they have never fully recovered . . .

It occurs to me that I attract the mentally unbalanced. Or perhaps
their therapists have advised them to take up outdoor work? There
was the beautiful young Italian, a veritable Donatello with black
curly hair and a bronze torso we saw a lot of because he liked to bare
it while he worked. He arrived in a Cadillac of immense size, did
little work but talked a lot about trips he intended to make,
businesses he meant to start, and often asked to use the telephone.
He was eventually arrested for having tried to murder his mistress,
and though he was given a suspended sentence it seemed better not
to have him around . . .

B.B. was a machinist, not a nurseryman or an arborist; and that has been true of all my helpers. They all belong to the ranks of the temporarily unemployed or they are moonlighting. Not one of them has ever had the slightest knowledge of horticulture, or ever acquired it – not even my dear A.V., with me for five years, who truly did love the garden . . . but never learned to identify a single flower, bush or tree or any of the techniques connected with growing them.

ELEANOR PERÉNYI,
Green Thoughts, 1982

Some gardeners fight with their gardens. Every day brings a new struggle. But the best-loved books are by gardeners with a more relaxed attitude, like Mrs Margery Fish, who could communicate to her readers both her passion for plants and her rare gift for grouping them. This was instinctive, and when she writes that she 'happened' to plant two or three things together which associated well, that is just the right word, and much more encouraging than constant exhortations to plan, weed, spray, draw up a programme, and generally turn pleasure into pain. In short, she makes it sound easy.

Another very good mixer is a very plebeian plant, *Pimpernella major rosea*, which is nothing more than a pink cow parsley. Ferny leaves and rather dull pink flowers are a good foil for any strong-coloured or bold plant. I happened to plant it near the deep blue *Campanula glomerata*, with its clustered heads, and both plants are better for the association. I have never given much thought to the cow parsley and was rather shaken when a visitor from a distance who spent a long time doing the garden, told me at the end of the tour that seeing the cow parsley had made his day and he would have come any distance to see it! It made me feel unappreciative and I went back to look at it spreading its delicate leaves under the Judas tree, and in another place where it was growing with *Polemonium caeruleum* and the striped grass, *Phalaris arundinacea variegata*, with a blue cedar as background.

It is always a great pleasure – and surprise – when you happen on just the perfect place in which to plant some special treasure.

MARGERY FISH,
A Flower for Every Day, 1965

Christopher Lloyd is another tolerant gardener, even with pests, if they are decorative.

I am very fond of moorhens. They can get away with some pretty heinous crimes, as far as I am concerned. Time was when we used to shoot any that appeared on the scene and eat them in moorhen pies . . .

But as fast as you shoot moorhens, others will come in from the neighbouring countryside. No piece of water with vegetation in and around it will be left untenanted for any length of time. All you will succeed in doing is to make them into exceedingly scary birds, on the point of disappearing even as you first espy them and always making you feel a brute – which is just about what you are. Ours, which have now remained unmolested for fifteen or twenty years, are for the most part tame enough to treat us as so much garden furniture. It is a real delight to sit down by the horse pond and watch them about their business, strutting deliberately across the waterlily pads and prodding to right and to left, or marshalling their young, which are the tiniest balls of black fluff, apparently blown about the water's surface.

CHRISTOPHER LLOYD,
The Well-Tempered Garden, 1970

'My verse is always about places,' says John Betjeman of his poetry, but it is always about feelings, too. Here, the scene and the girl are absurd, but the feelings are real.

POT POURRI FROM A SURREY GARDEN

Miles of pram in the wind and Pam in the gorse track,
    Coco-nut smell of the broom, and a packet of Weights
Press'd in the sand. The thud of a hoof on a horse-track –
    A horse-riding horse for a horse-track –
    Conifer county of Surrey approached
Through remarkable wrought-iron gates.

Over your boundary now, I wash my face in a bird-bath,
    Then which path shall I take? that over there by the pram?
Down by the pond! or – yes, I will take the slippery third path,
    Trodden away with gym shoes,
    Beautiful fir-dry alley that leads
To the bountiful body of Pam.

Pam, I adore you, Pam, you great mountainous sports girl,
    Whizzing them over the net, full of the strength of five:
That old Malvernian brother, you zephyr and khaki shorts girl,
    Although he's playing for Woking,
    Can't stand up
To your wonderful backhand drive.

See the strength of her arm, as firm and hairy as Hendren's;
    See the size of her thighs, the pout of her lips as, cross,
And full of a pent-up strength, she swipes at the rhododendrons,
    Lucky the rhododendrons,
    And flings her arrogant love-lock
Back with a petulant toss.

Over the redolent pinewoods, in at the bathroom casement,
  One fine Saturday, Windlesham bells shall call:
Up the Butterfield aisle rich with Gothic enlacement,
  Licensed now for embracement,
  Pam and I, as the organ
Thunders over you all.

JOHN BETJEMAN,
Old Lights for New Chancels, 1940

This is a favourite song of John Betjeman's, who was a keen frequenter of music-halls in his youth. It is nice to read something poetic about a town garden, even if it's rather sad.

If you saw my little back-yard, 'Wot a pretty spot!' you'd cry —
It's a picture on a sunny summer day,
Wiv the turnip-tops and cabbages wot people's doesn't buy
I makes it on a Sunday look all gay.
The neighbours fink I grow 'em and you'd fancy you're in Kent,
Or at Epsom if you gaze into the mews —
It's a wonder as the landlord doesn't want to raise the rent,
Because we've got such nobby distant views.

    Oh it really is a wery pretty garden,
    And Chingford to the eastward could be seen;
    Wiv a ladder and some glasses,
    You could see to 'Ackney Marshes,
    If it wasn't for the 'ouses in between.

We're as countrified as can be wiv a clothes-prop for a tree,
The tub-stool makes a rustic little stile;
Every time the blooming clock strikes there's a cuckoo sings to
    me,
And I've painted up 'To Leather Lane a mile.'
Wiv tomatoes and wiv radishes wot 'adn't any sale,
The backyard looks a puffick mass o' bloom;
And I've made a little bee-hive wiv some beetles in a pail,
And a pitchfork wiv the handle of a broom.

    Oh! it really is a wery pretty garden,
    And Rye 'Ouse from the cockloft could be seen;
    Where the chickweed man undresses,
    To bathe among the watercresses,
    If it wasn't for the 'ouses in between . . .

Though the gas-works isn't wilet, they improve the rural scene —
For mountains they would very nicely pass;
There's the mushrooms in the dust-hole, with the cowcumbers
    so green —
It only wants a bit o' 'ot-house glass.
I wears this milkman's nightshirt, and I sits outside all day,
Like the ploughboy cove what's mizzled o'er the Lea;
And when I goes indoors at night they dunno what I say,
'Cause my language gets as yokel as can be.

    Oh! it really is a wery pretty garden,
    And soap-works from the 'ousetops could be seen;
    If I got a rope and pulley,
    I'd enjoy the breeze more fully
    If it wasn't for the 'ouses in between.

EDGAR BATEMAN,
The Cockney's Garden, 1894, sung by Gus Elen

It's comforting to find how wrong that great polymath, Ruskin, could be; wrong about his own time, wrong about the past, and wrong about the future.

Perhaps, it may be thought, if we understood flowers better, we might love them less.

We do not love them much, as it is. Few people really care about flowers. Many, indeed, are fond of finding a new shape of blossom, caring for it as a child cares about a kaleidoscope. Many, also, like a fair service of flowers in the greenhouse, as a fair service of plate on the table. Many are scientifically interested in them, though even these in the nomenclature rather than the flowers. And a few enjoy their gardens: but I have never heard of a piece of land, which would let well on a building lease, remaining unlet because it was a flowery piece. I have never heard of parks being kept for wild hyacinths, though often of their being kept for wild beasts. And the blossoming time of the year being principally spring, I perceive it to be the mind of most people, during that period, to stay in towns.

JOHN RUSKIN,
Modern Painters, Vol. 5, 1860

Not all romantics are in search of human love, and among my heroes are those other romantics, the plant collectors, the men who spent years in the untrodden places of the world looking for unknown species in the interests of science, or from a sheer love of flowers. The dangers and hardships were extraordinary, but so were the compensations — the beauty of the forests and mountains, the thrill of discovery, the happy companionships. For sheer enthusiasm, Frank Kingdon Ward, plant collector, geologist and mountaineer, must take the palm.

A born traveller, he spent ten years in the heart of Asia exploring Burma, India and China in plant habitats ranging from black jungles to snow-covered Himalayan peaks. His object was threefold: to collect seeds of hardy flowering plants for English gardens, to collect dried specimens for study, and to explore unknown mountain ranges. He was supremely successful in each endeavour, particularly in the collection of hundreds of rhododendrons. He took great delight in his work, and enjoyed not only the capture of rare plants, but also the overwhelming beauty of the flowers in their masses in the wild scenery. The first of these two extracts is about Burma, where he was camping at 11,000 feet, the second about West China.

I am sitting by the fire in my log hut in the Seinghku valley. A keen wind is blowing through the chinks and crannies but wrapped in a long woollen *chupa*, by the fire, sipping a nightcap of rum and hot water, I do not feel the cold. From outside comes only the shrill voice of the stream bubbling over the stones, and the occasional clatter of falling rocks high up on the screes; otherwise it is very still. By ten o'clock I am yawning, and having written up my diary, I prepare to turn in. But first I take a look round outside to see that all is well. The fine mist which usually fills the air after dark has disappeared and the sky is riddled with stars. Far down the valley a scimitar moon is being withdrawn slowly from a scabbard of cloud. 'Tomorrow it will be fine,' I say to myself, stamping my feet, for at 11,000 feet altitude it is chilly at night even in July, and there is much snow higher up the valley; 'I will go for a big climb'; and with that pleasant thought I crawl between the blankets and snuggle down for the night.

FRANK KINGDON WARD,
Plant Hunting on the Edge of the World, 1930

By mid-June the marshes which fringe the plain are a tumult of blossom. Here *Primula poissonii* grows to perfection, and it must be confessed that, despite its aggressive colour – screaming magenta purple – in mass formation it is a gay sight. There is something in the velvet texture of the corolla which gives a purer colour value in the sunshine. Nature, too, comes to the rescue. Boldly she meets violence with violence, loud colour with louder contrast, outdaring man. Thus she plants with *P. poissonii* the marsh kingcup, whose hot gold serves as a foil to belligerent purple. The effect is wondrous; and when to these are added splashes of sky-blue Cynoglossum and of pink lousewort, the wild bog garden is an unforgettable splendour.

FRANK KINGDON WARD,
The Romance of Plant Hunting, 1924

Few of the plant hunters impart the excitement of discovery more vividly than Reginald Farrer, the best writer of them all, though others surpassed him as a collector. Farrer travelled deep into north-west China in 1914, where he found the theatrically beautiful Paeonia moutan, *which had for long been known in Chinese gardens, growing wild. No discovery of gold or treasure, or even of a lost city, could be more thrilling.*

Through the foaming shallows of the copse I plunged, and soon was holding my breath with growing excitement as I neared my goal, and it became more and more certain that I was setting eyes on *Paeonia moutan* as a wild plant. The event itself justified enthusiasm, but all considerations of botanical geography vanish from one's mind in the first contemplation of that amazing flower, the most overpoweringly superb of hardy shrubs. Here in the brushwood it grew up tall and slender and straight, in two or three unbranching shoots, each one of which carried at the top, elegantly balancing, that single enormous blossom, waved and crimped into the boldest grace of line, of absolute pure white, with featherings of deepest maroon radiating at the base of the petals from the boss of golden fluff at the flower's heart. Above the sere and thorny scrub the snowy beauties poise and hover, and the breath of them went out upon the twilight as sweet as any rose. For a long time I remained in worship, and returned downwards at last in the dusk in high contentment.

REGINALD FARRER,
On the Eaves of the World, 1917

One plant hunter lacked the magic spark, and I always think of him as
'poor' David Douglas. He was a successful collector, particularly of conifers,
but not a lucky one, and he did not seem to relish his adventures, as did
Farrer and Kingdon Ward, or to be blessed with their stamina. Collecting
in western North America, he suffered from rheumatism, bad feet, agues,
accidents and low spirits, and often lost his collections in raging rivers or
had to eat them through hunger. He was later killed by a wild bull while
collecting in Hawaii, at the early age of thirty-five. Here are a few pathetic
extracts from his journal, which records only the hardships of plant-collecting
with none of the compensations of romance. I think of David Douglas with
a twinge of guilt whenever I am enjoying my little patch of the pretty yellow-
and-white annual, Limnanthes douglasii.

1825. It rained both days. We used all the berries I had collected on
this journey, and Mr McKenzie suffered some inconvenience from
having eaten a few roots of a species of *Narthecium*.

1826. I descended the whole chain of the river from the Kettle Falls
to the sea, a distance of 800 miles, 600 of that in Indian canoes. In
the narrow part below the Great Falls, a dangerous rapid part of the
river, my canoe was wrecked . . . Melancholy to relate, I lost the
whole of my insects, a few seeds, and my pistols.

. . . I had left my new guide at the camp and proceeded in a south-
east direction, and had only crossed a low hill when I came to
abundance of *Pinus lambertiana*. I put myself in possession of a great
number of perfect cones, but circumstances obliged me to leave the
ground hastily with only three – a party of eight Indians endeavoured
to destroy me.

. . . We returned nearly by the same way we had come, in twelve
days' hard labour, with great misery, hunger, rain and cold;
but what gave me most pain was the nearly total loss of my

collections crossing the River Sandiam, one of the tributaries of
the Multnomah.

DAVID DOUGLAS,
*Journal During His Travels
in North America*, 1823–7

When I made my will some years ago I directed that my funeral should be as simple and economical as possible, and that my ashes should be scattered, if convenient, over the garden of my country cottage. I little knew in what illustrious footsteps I was treading. Sir William Temple, courtier, diplomatist, philosopher and gardening writer in the seventeenth century, laid this down in his will in 1695.

I desire my body may be interred at Westminster Abbey near those two dear pledges gone before me but with as much privacy and as small expense as my executors shall find convenient. And I desire and appoint that my heart may be interred six foot underground on the South East side of the stone dial in my little garden at Moreparke.

WILLIAM TEMPLE,
1695

This epitaph was engraved on the tomb in Lambeth of the three John Tradescants, great gardeners of the early seventeenth century. The second Tradescant hunted plants in Europe and Russia. The youngest sailed three times to the New World and brought home many exciting introductions, including the scarlet runner bean. Tradescant's Ark in Lambeth, rich in collections of plants, minerals, shells, coins, fishes and other curiosities, including a dodo, was one of the sights of London.

Know, stranger, ere thou pass, beneath this stone
Lye John Tradescant, grandsire, father, son.
The last died in his spring — the other two
Liv'd till they had travell'd Art and Nature through:
As by their choice collections may appear
Of what is rare, in land, in sea, in air.
Whilst they (as Homer's Illiad in a nut)
A world of wonders in one closet shut.
These famous Antiquarians that had been
Both gardeners to the Rose and Lily Queen,
Transplanted now themselves, sleep here, and when
Angels shall with their trumpets waken men
And fire shall purge the world, these hence shall rise,
And change this garden for a Paradise.

This verse from The Land *was printed on the service-sheet at Vita's funeral.*

She walks among the loveliness she made,
Between the apple-blossom and the water —
She walks among the patterned pied brocade,
Each flower her son and every tree her daughter.

V. SACKVILLE-WEST,
The Land, 1926

At first sight, Disraeli's tastes seem unashamedly gorgeous, in clothes, parties, food, houses, language, servants, parks and gardens. When his hero Lothair celebrates his coming of age, he gives a princely party at his vast hereditary seat, Muriel Towers. He is met on arrival by a cavalcade of 500 horsemen, and gradually a house-party assembles consisting of dukes and duchesses, bishops, monsignori and a cardinal, exquisite young ladies of title and bored young aristocrats who have come for the shooting. After touring the great galleries and saloons and glancing casually at the pictures and treasures beyond price, the guests are taken out of doors. Though Disraeli is fascinated at the splendour he has conjured up, he is laughing at it all the same.

After luncheon they visited the gardens, which had been formed in a sylvan valley enclosed by gilded gates. The creator of this paradise had been favoured by nature, and had availed himself of this opportunity. The contrast between the parterres blazing with colour and the sylvan background, the undulating paths over romantic heights, the fanes and the fountains, the glittering statues, and the Babylonian terraces, formed a whole much of which was beautiful, and all of which was striking and singular.

'Perhaps too many temples,' said Lothair.

BENJAMIN DISRAELI,
Lothair, 1870

Did Disraeli at heart prefer a garden of old-fashioned flowers to blazing parterres? Lady Corisande's garden, quite free from Victorian ostentation, would make one think so.

It was about a week after the arrival of Lothair, and they were at breakfast at Brentham, in that bright room full of little round tables which Lothair always admired, looking, as it did, upon a garden of many colours.

'How I hate modern gardens,' said St Aldegonde. 'What a horrid thing this is! One might as well have a mosaic pavement there. Give me cabbage-roses, sweet-peas, and wallflowers. That is my idea of a garden. Corisande's garden is the only sensible thing of the sort.'

'One likes a mosaic pavement to look like a garden,' said Euphrosyne, 'but not a garden like a mosaic pavement.' . . .

It was agreed that after breakfast they should go and see Corisande's garden. And a party did go: all the Phoebus family, and Lord and Lady St Aldegonde, and Lady Corisande, and Bertram and Lothair.

In the pleasure-grounds of Brentham were the remains of an ancient garden of the ancient house that had long ago been pulled down. When the modern pleasure-grounds were planned and created, notwithstanding the protests of the artists in landscape, the father of the present Duke would not allow this ancient garden to be entirely destroyed, and you came upon its quaint appearance in the dissimilar world in which it was placed, as you might in some festival of romantic costume upon a person habited in the courtly dress of the last century. It was formed upon a gentle southern slope, with turfen terraces walled in on three sides, the fourth consisting of arches of golden yew. The Duke had given this garden to Lady Corisande, in order that she might practise her theory, that flower-gardens should be sweet and luxuriant, and not hard and scentless imitations of works of art. Here, in their season, flourished abundantly all those productions of nature which are now banished from our once delighted senses: huge bushes of honeysuckle, and bowers of sweet-pea and sweetbriar and jessamine clustering over the walls, and gillyflowers scenting with their sweet breath the ancient bricks from which they seemed to spring. There were banks of violets which the southern breeze always stirred, and mignonette filled every vacant nook. As they entered now, it seemed a blaze of roses and carnations, though one recognized in a moment the presence of the lily, the heliotrope, and the stock. Some white peacocks were basking on the southern wall, and one of them, as their visitors entered, moved and displayed its plumage with scornful pride. The bees were busy in the air, but their homes were near, and you might watch them labouring in their glassy hives.

BENJAMIN DISRAELI,
Lothair, 1870

Two conflicting views of country life:

God the first garden made, and the first city, Cain.

ABRAHAM COWLEY,
The Garden, c. 1666

My view of the countryside has always been that it would be better for an ample covering of asphalt, and of flowers that they are things found in florists, for giving to pretty ladies.

BERNARD LEVIN,
The Times, 11 April 1974

This is one of the earliest descriptions of a cottage garden, from Chaucer, who died in 1400. The garden was merely a yard, with poultry, vegetables, and a good stock of medicinal herbs. The hero of the Nun's Priest's Tale is Chanticleer, a fine cock, who falls ill, and, like human husbands, makes a tremendous fuss and claims he is dying. His chief wife, Pertelote, diagnoses constipation, and prescribes herbal purges from the garden.

Once, long ago, there dwelt a poor old widow
In a small cottage, by a little meadow
Beside a grove and standing in a dale.
This widow-woman of whom I tell my tale
Since the sad day when last she was a wife
Had led a very patient, simple life.
Little she had in capital or rent,
But still, by making do with what God sent,
She kept herself and her two daughters going.
Three hefty sows — no more — were all her showing,
Three cows as well; there was a sheep called Molly.
　　Sooty her hall, her kitchen melancholy . . .

　　She had a yard that was enclosed about
By a stockade and a dry ditch without,
In which she kept a cock called Chanticleer.
In all the land for crowing he'd no peer;
His voice was jollier than the organ blowing
In church on Sundays, he was great at crowing.
Far, far more regular than any clock
Or abbey bell the crowing of this cock . . .

Then Chanticleer began to have bad dreams and screaming fits, and Pertelote dosed him herself.

'I shall myself instruct you and prescribe
Herbs that will cure all vapours of the tribe,

Herbs from our very farmyard! You will find
Their natural property is to unbind . . .
Worms for a day or two I'll have to give
As a digestive, then your laxative.
Centaury, fumitory, caper-spurge
And hellebore will make a splendid purge;
And then there's laurel or the blackthorn berry,
Ground-ivy too that makes our yard so merry;
Peck them right up, my dear, and swallow
    whole.
Be happy, husband, by your father's soul.'

GEOFFREY CHAUCER,
The Canterbury Tales,
translated into modern English
by Nevill Coghill

What a world of difference there is between the poor widow's garden in Chaucer and the postmistress's cottage garden in Candleford Green in the 1880s, crammed with ferns and flowers. But how much is idealized in Flora Thompson's memory? The trilogy Lark Rise to Candleford *is a masterpiece, and a goldmine for the social historian, but is it not sometimes too sweet, are the old village ladies not too kindly and apple-cheeked, did the old-fashioned flowers never succumb to bug or blight?*

She had been in that garden before, but never in May, with the apple blossom out and the wallflowers filling the air with their fragrance.

Narrow paths between high, built-up banks supporting flower borders, crowded with jonquils, auriculas, forget-me-nots and other spring flowers, led from one part of the garden to another. One winding path led to the earth closet in its bower of nut-trees halfway down the garden, another to the vegetable garden and on to the rough grass plot before the beehives. Between each section were thick groves of bushes with ferns and capers and Solomon's seal, so closed in that the long, rough grass there was always damp. Wasted ground, a good gardener might have said, but delightful in its cool, green shadiness.

Nearer the house was a portion given up entirely to flowers, not growing in beds or borders, but crammed together in an irregular square, where they bloomed in half-wild profusion. There were rose bushes there and lavender and rosemary and a bush apple-tree which bore little red and yellow streaked apples in later summer, and Michaelmas daisies and red-hot pokers and old-fashioned pompom dahlias in autumn and peonies and pinks already budding.

An old man in the village came one day a week to till the vegetable garden, but the flower garden was no one's especial business. Miss Lane herself would occasionally pull on a pair of wash-leather gloves and transplant a few seedlings; Matthew would pull up a weed or stake a plant as he passed, and the smiths, once a year, turned out of the shop to dig between the roots and cut down dead canes.

Betweenwhiles the flowers grew just as they would in crowded masses, perfect in their imperfection.

FLORA THOMPSON,
Candleford Green, 1943

All the writings of Colette are permeated with a love of animals and plants and all the beauties and mysteries of the country. This she inherited from her adored mother, 'Sido', who was a magical gardener blessed with both an artist's eye and strong working hands. 'Why,' wrote Colette, 'did no one ever model or paint or carve that hand of Sido's, tanned and wrinkled early by household tasks, gardening, cold water and the sun, with its long, finely-tapering fingers and its beautiful, convex, oval nails?' The family house and garden were in a village in Lower Burgundy, where Colette spent her childhood and to which her thoughts returned often throughout her long life. The garden blossomed with wisteria and roses, hydrangeas and double red violets, sweet peas and lupins, geraniums and succulents in pots, bore walnuts and cherries and bush fruit in abundance, and had a fenced-off kitchen garden and poultry-yard.

Colette recalls that the garden glowed in summer with warm colours.

It was the reflected glow of your blazing line along the terrace, O geraniums, and yours, O foxgloves, springing up amidst the coppice, that gave my childish cheeks their rosy warmth. For Sido loved red and pink in the garden, the burning shades of roses, lychnis, hydrangeas and red-hot pokers. She even loved the winter-cherry, although she declared that its pulpy pink flowers, veined with red, reminded her of the lights of a freshly killed calf. She made a reluctant pact with the East wind. 'I know how to get on with him,' she would say. But she remained suspicious and, out of all the cardinal and collateral points of the compass, it was on that icy treacherous point, with its murderous pranks, that she kept her eye. But she trusted him with lily of the valley bulbs, some begonias, and mauve autumn crocuses, those dim lanterns of cold twilights.

Except for one mound with a clump of cherry-laurels overshadowed by a maiden-hair tree — whose skate-shaped leaves I used to give to my school friends to press between the pages of their atlases — the whole warm garden basked in a yellow light that shimmered into red and violet; but whether this red and violet sprang then, and still springs, from feelings of happiness or from dazzled sight, I could not tell.

COLETTE,
Sido, 1929

So individual and poetic is Colette's French, that I add the original.

O géraniums, ô digitales . . . Celles-ci fusant des bois-taillis, ceux-là en rampe allumés au long de la terrasse, c'est de votre reflet que ma joue d'enfant reçut un don vermeil. Car 'Sido' aimait au jardin le rouge, le rose, les sanguines filles du rosier, de la croix-de-Malte, des hortensias et des bâtons-de-Saint-Jacques, et même le coqueret-alkékenge, encore qu'elle accusât sa fleur, veinée de rouge sur pulpe rose, de lui rappeler un mou de veau frais. A contre-coeur elle faisait pacte avec l'Est: 'Je m'arrange avec lui,' disait-elle. Mais elle demeurait pleine de suspicion et surveillait, entre tous les cardinaux et collatéraux, ce point glacé, traître, aux jeux meurtriers. Elle lui confiait des bulbes de muguet, quelques bégonias, et des crocus mauves, veilleuses des froids crépuscules.

Hors une corne de terre, hors un bosquet de lauriers-cerises dominés par un junko-biloba – je donnais ses feuilles, en forme de raie, à mes camarades d'école, qui les séchaient entre les pages de l'atlas – tout le chaud jardin se nourrissait d'une lumière jaune, à tremblements rouges et violets, mais je ne pourrais dire si ce rouge, ce violet dépendaient, dépendent encore d'un sentimental bonheur ou d'un éblouissement optique.

The tradition of the parson-gardener is centuries old, and some of them were
attractive characters. One of the most delightful was the poet, the Rev.
George Crabbe, a self-taught botanist whose first garden was in Suffolk, his
second in Rutland. Though his taste was for botanic gardening, he admired
the skill and enthusiasm of the florists — the artisans whose absorbing hobby
was breeding flowers for exhibition. He wrote of one in The Borough, *the*
long poem which includes the story of Peter Grimes.

It is good to know that when Crabbe arrived in London as a young man,
desperate and destitute, he was given an instant welcome by Edmund Burke,
a total stranger to whom he had sent his poems.

There is my friend the Weaver; strong desires
Reign in his breast; 'tis beauty he admires: . . .
For him is blooming in its rich array
The glorious flower which bore the palm away;
In vain a rival tried his utmost art,
His was the prize, and joy o'erflow'd his heart.
   'This, this is beauty! cast, I pray, your eyes
On this my glory! see the grace! the size!
Was ever stem so tall, so stout, so strong,
Exact in breadth, in just proportion, long!
These brilliant hues are all distinct and clean,
No kindred tint, no blending streaks between;
This is no shaded, run-off, pin-eyed thing,
A king of flowers, a flower for England's king:
I own my pride, and thank the favouring star,
Which shed such beauty on my fair Bizarre.'
   Thus may the poor the cheap indulgence seize,
While the most wealthy pine and pray for ease.

THE REV. GEORGE CRABBE,
The Borough, 1810

Of the many parson-gardeners of Victorian times one of the most accomplished was Canon Henry Ellacombe, Vicar of Bitton in Gloucestershire, plant collector, Shakespearian scholar, amateur architect and champion of the 'natural' garden. His parsonage garden dripped with old roses, his walls were smothered in climbers, and his flower-beds were full of plant species, old-fashioned flowers and plants with beautiful leaves. He also had a well-trained family, for it was his custom to rest on a couch before dinner and compose Latin verses which he read to them during the meal.

From his book about his garden (which was much visited by gardening celebrities) I have chosen a piece describing its importance in his parish work.

The love of flowers is so universal, and the garden may be such a useful adjunct to the cottage, yet there is very great ignorance of the right principles of gardening, and the parson may be of great use to his poorer neighbours, not only by teaching, but still more by showing them better ways in his own garden. For the parsonage garden gate should be always open, and every parishioner welcomed; there need be no fear of any undue advantage being taken of the free permission to enter – the one difficulty will be to induce them to come in. And the parson may do much to brighten the gardens of his parish, and so to increase the interest in them by giving plants from his own garden. I have for many years been a cultivator of hardy plants, and have been able to gather together a large number of species; and I was long ago taught, and have always held, that it is impossible to get or keep a large collection except by constant liberality in giving.

CANON HENRY ELLACOMBE,
In a Gloucestershire Garden, 1895

At last! Even the confirmed townee comes round to it in time.

Should you happen to come across me in the near future and hear me muttering things like 'Sheep nesting high this year, 'twill be a hard winter', or 'Blossom on bough, go milk a cow', or 'I don't hold wi' all this manure on the land – 'tis against nature – give me Fisons every time', please evince no surprise. The fact is, I have acquired a window box and gone spectacularly horticultural overnight.

BERNARD LEVIN,
Taking Sides, 1979

Two views of the rose . . .

   The old Persian poets praise taverns more often than gardens, and the grape more than the rose, but there is one lovely line about the rose in Omar Khayyam.

Look to the Rose that blows about us — 'Lo,
Laughing,' she says, 'into the World I blow;
   At once the silken Tassel of my Purse
Tear, and its Treasure on the Garden throw.'

OMAR KHAYYAM,
The Rubaiyat, translated by Edward Fitzgerald, 1859

Another rose verse is by a modern poet, Ralph Hodgson, so full of paradox that when I first saw it, without a provenance, I thought it was seventeenth century.

THE ROSE

How praise the rose! Let praise go by:
Let us not praise where praising were
To underpraise; we may come nigh,
Withholding praise, to praising her.

RALPH HODGSON,
Collected Poems, 1961

Two views of the geranium . . .
   Miss Mitford of Our Village *was a dab hand with geraniums and grew them in a wire pyramid in the garden room in winter, out of doors in summer. She takes a sensible spinster's view of the plant.*

Such geraniums! It does not become us poor mortals to be vain — but, really, my geraniums! There is certainly nothing but the garden into which Aladdin found his way, and where the fruit was composed of gems, that can compare with them. This pyramid is undoubtedly the great object from the greenhouse.

MISS MARY MITFORD,
Our Village, 1824–32

Thomas Erskine's poem on the geranium is highly erotic. It has for long been attributed to Sheridan, but after much burrowing in libraries I have come to the conclusion that it is by his friend, Thomas Erskine. I wait with trepidation for scholars to shoot me down.

In the close covert of a grove,
By nature formed for scenes of love,
Said Susan in a lucky hour,
Observe yon sweet geranium flower;
How straight upon its stalk it stands,
And tempts our violating hands:
Whilst the soft bud as yet unspread,
Hangs down its pale declining head:
Yet, soon as it is ripe to blow,
The stems shall rise, the head shall glow.
Nature, said I, my lovely Sue,
To all her followers lends a clue;
Her simple laws themselves explain,
As links of one continued chain;
For her the mysteries of creation,
Are but the works of generation:
Yon blushing, strong, triumphant flower,
Is in the crisis of its power:
But short, alas! its vigorous reign,
He sheds his seed, and drops again;
The bud that hangs in pale decay,
Feels, not, as yet, the plastic ray;
Tomorrow's sun shall bid him rise,
Then, too, he sheds his seed and dies:
But words, my love, are vain and weak,
For proof, let bright example speak;

Then straight before the wondering maid,
The tree of life I gently laid;
Observe, sweet Sue, his drooping head,
How pale, how languid, and how dead;
Yet, let the sun of thy bright eyes,
Shine but a moment, it shall rise;
Let but the dew of thy soft hand
Refresh the stem, it straight shall stand:
Already, see, it swells, it grows,
Its head is redder than the rose,
Its shrivelled fruit, of dusky hue,
Now glows, a present fit for Sue:
The balm of life each artery fills,
And in o'erflowing drops distils.
Oh me! cried Susan, when is this?
What strange tumultuous throbs of bliss!
Sure, never mortal, till this hour,
Felt such emotion at a flower:
Oh, serpent! cunning to deceive,
Sure, 'tis this tree that tempted Eve;
The crimson apples hang so fair,
Alas! what woman could forbear?
Well, hast thou guessed, my love, I cried,
It is the tree by which she died;
The tree which could content her,
All nature, Susan, seeks the centre;
Yet, let us still, poor Eve forgive,
It's the tree by which we live . . .

THE HON. THOMAS ERSKINE

Two views of the tulip . . .

Who ever said the Dutch were a sensible race? Their passion for breeding tulips in the early seventeenth century degenerated into such wild speculation in bulbs that the nation nearly went bankrupt.

The highest prices paid by tulip speculators bore no possible relation to the beauty of the flower. For one 'Viceroy' bulb, paid for in kind, the following goods were given: 2 loads of wheat; 4 loads of rye; 4 fat oxen; 8 fat pigs; 12 fat sheep; 2 hogsheads of wine; 4 barrels of 8-florin beer; 2 barrels of butter; 1,000 lb of cheese; a complete bed; a suit of clothes and a silver beaker – the whole valued at 2,500 florins. One bulb of 'Semper Augustus' fetched nearly twice that sum, together with a fine new carriage and pair.

WILFRID BLUNT,
Tulipomania, 1950

'The Tulip Chief' of eighteenth-century Turkey loved his tulips for their beauty rather than their cash value. Wilfrid Blunt tells us that he wrote a book about them naming more than thirteen hundred varieties, with lyrical descriptions such as this.

She has the colour of the violet, and the curved form of the new moon. Her markings are rightly placed, clean, and well-proportioned. Her shape is like the almond, needle-like, and ornamented with pleasant rays. Her inner petals are like a well, as they should be; her outer petals a little open, this too as it should be. The white, ornamented petals are absolutely perfect. She is the chosen of the chosen.

THE SHEIKH MOHAMMED LALÉZARÉ

Sometimes, in his childhood, Proust's aunt Léonie would give him a fragment of a madeleine soaked in real or lime-flower tea, and in later life the memory of the taste of the tea and madeleine would stir in his mind a long chain of recollections of his life at Combray. 'The smell and taste of things remain poised for a long time, like souls, ready to remind us, waiting and hoping for their moment, amid the ruins of all the rest.'

If some childhood scenes were conjured up by the sense of taste, the sense of smell was equally evocative, and, recalling the scents of flowers and gardens, Proust would remember the walks he took with his father and grandfather from the house at Combray along the 'Méséglise way' and the 'Guermantes way'. The Méséglise way went by M. Swann's park, and often a detour had to be taken if M. Swann's 'unsuitable' wife was known to be at home; but when she was away, they could enjoy the park.

When we had decided to go the 'Méséglise way' we would start (without undue haste, and even if the sky were clouded over, since the walk was not very long, and did not take us too far from home), as though we were not going anywhere in particular, by the front-door of my aunt's house, which opened on to the Rue du Saint-Esprit. We would be greeted by the gunsmith, we would drop our letters into the box, we would tell Théodore, from Françoise, as we passed, that she had run out of oil or coffee, and we would leave the town by the road which ran along the white fence of M. Swann's park. Before reaching it we would be met on our way by the scent of his lilac-trees, come out to welcome strangers. Out of the fresh little green hearts of their foliage the lilacs raised inquisitively over the fence of the park their plumes of white or purple blossom, which glowed, even in the shade, with the sunlight in which they had been bathed. Some of them, half-concealed by the little tiled house, called the Archers' Lodge, in which Swann's keeper lived, overtopped its gothic gable with their rosy minaret. The nymphs of spring would have seemed coarse and vulgar in comparison with these young houris, who retained, in this French garden, the pure and vivid

colouring of a Persian miniature. Despite my desire to throw my
arms about their pliant forms and to draw down towards me the
starry locks that crowned their fragrant heads, we would pass them
by without stopping, for my parents had ceased to visit Tansonville
since Swann's marriage, and, so as not to appear to be looking into
his park, we would, instead of taking the road which ran beside its
boundary and then climbed straight up to the open fields, choose
another way, which led in the same direction, but circuitously, and
brought us out rather too far from home.

One day my grandfather said to my father: 'Don't you remember
Swann's telling us yesterday that his wife and daughter had gone off
to Rheims and that he was taking the opportunity of spending a day
or two in Paris? We might go along by the park, since the ladies are
not at home; that will make it a little shorter.'

We stopped for a moment by the fence. Lilac-time was nearly
over; some of the trees still thrust aloft, in tall purple chandeliers,
their tiny balls of blossom, but in many places among their foliage
where, only a week before, they had still been breaking in waves of
fragrant foam, these were now spent and shrivelled and discoloured,
a hollow scum, dry and scentless.

*The 'Guermantes way' would impress the young walker quite differently, for
the Guermantes family ranked high in the aristocracy of France, their
ancestors emblazoned in the windows of the Combray church.*

And then it happened that, going the 'Guermantes way', I passed
occasionally by a row of well-watered little gardens, over whose
hedges rose clusters of dark blossom. I would stop before them,
hoping to gain some precious addition to my experience, for I seemed
to have before my eyes a fragment of that riverside country which I
had longed so much to see and know since coming upon a description
of it by one of my favourite authors. And it was with that story-book
land, with its imagined soil intersected by a hundred bubbling
water-courses, that Guermantes, changing its form in my mind,
became identified, after I heard Dr Percepied speak of the flowers

and the charming rivulets and fountains that were to be seen there
in the ducal park. I used to dream that Mme de Guermantes, taking
a sudden capricious fancy for myself, invited me there, that all day
long she stood fishing for trout by my side. And when evening came,
holding my hand in her own, as we passed by the little gardens of
her vassals, she would point out to me the flowers that leaned their
red and purple spikes along the tops of the low walls, and would
teach me all their names.

*Though the two walks from Combray were so different and led, in
recollection, to different chains of thought, both the Méséglise and the
Guermantes ways were fixed in Proust's imagination by the smell of flowers.*

No doubt, by virtue of having permanently and indissolubly
combined in me groups of different impressions, for no reason save
that they had made me feel several separate things at the same time,
the Méséglise and Guermantes 'ways' left me exposed, in later life,
to much disillusionment, and even to many mistakes. For often I
have wished to see a person again without realizing that it was simply
because that person recalled to me a hedge of hawthorns in blossom;
and I have been led to believe, and to make some one else believe in
an aftermath of affection, by what was no more than an inclination
to travel. But by the same qualities, and by their persistence in those
of my impressions, today, to which they can find an attachment, the
two 'ways' give to those impressions a foundation, depth, a dimension
lacking from the rest. They invest them, too, with a charm, a
significance which is for me alone. When, on a summer evening, the
resounding sky growls like a tawny lion, and everyone is complaining
of the storm, it is along the 'Méséglise way' that my fancy strays
alone in ecstasy, inhaling, through the noise of falling rain, the
odour of invisible and persistent lilac-trees.

MARCEL PROUST,
Remembrance of Things Past. I.
Swann's Way, 1913, translated by
C. K. Scott Moncrieff

Soil and its food, in common parlance manure, are the very stuff of gardening. All sensible gardening writers praise manure, the garden's larder, but not many do it in verse.

Of composts shall the Muse descend to sing,
Nor soil her heavenly plumes? The sacred Muse
Naught sordid deems, but what is base; naught fair
Unless true Virtue stamp it with her seal.
Then, planter, wouldst thou double thy estate
Never, ah, never, be asham'd to tread
Thy dung-heaps.

JAMES GRAINGER, M.D.
(1721–70)

Karel Čapek chose to be witty about the serious business of soil creation.

Some people say that charcoal should be added, and others deny it; some recommend a dash of yellow sand, because it is supposed to contain iron, while others warn you against it for the very fact that it does contain iron. Others, again, recommend clean river sand, others peat alone, and still others sawdust. In short, the preparation

of the soil for seeds is a great mystery and a magic ritual. To it should be added marble dust (but where to get it?), three-year-old cow dung (here it is not clear whether it should be the dung of a three-year-old cow or a three-year-old heap), a handful from a fresh molehill, clay pounded to dust from old pigskin boots, sand from the Elbe (but not from the Vltava), three-year-old hotbed soil, and perhaps besides the humus from the golden fern and a handful from the grave of a hanged virgin — all that should be well mixed (gardening books do not say whether at the new moon, or full, or on midsummer night); and when you put this mysterious soil into flower-pots (soaked in water, which for three years have been standing in the sun, and on whose bottoms you put pieces of boiled crockery, and a piece of charcoal, against the use of which other authorities, of course, express their opinions) — when you have done all that, and so obeyed hundreds of prescriptions, principally contradicting each other, you may begin the real business of sowing the seeds.

KAREL ČAPEK,
The Gardener's Year, 1931

*The Persian poet, Omar Khayyam, writing in the early part of the twelfth
century, was familiar with the nutritional properties of dried blood.*

I sometimes think that never blows so red
The Rose as where some buried Caesar bled;
That every Hyacinth the Garden wears
Dropt in its Lap from some once lovely Head.

OMAR KHAYYAM,
The Rubaiyat,
translated by Edward Fitzgerald, 1859

There is a similar superstition in English flower lore, that Anemone
pulsatilla (Pulsatilla vulgaris) *grows only where Danish blood has flowed.*

Those of us who are used to handling chaste, sterilized bags of John Innes compost may recoil from the soil mixtures recommended by the auricula specialist, Isaac Emmerton, in 1815. The auricula was a 'florist's' flower, grown widely for exhibition. Some of Emmerton's rivals recoiled likewise, claiming that he overfed his plants, which were shortlived. Here are his favourite composts.

Compost, No. 1

3 Barrowsful of goose dung, steeped in bullock's blood,
3 Barrowsful of sugar-baker's scum,
2 Barrowsful of fine yellow loam.

Compost, No. 2

2 Barrowsful of goose dung, steeped in bullock's blood,
2 Barrowsful of sugar-baker's scum,
2 Barrowsful of night soil,
2 Barrowsful of fine yellow loam.

ISAAC EMMERTON,
Culture and Management of the Auricula, 1815

As always, Christopher Lloyd has his own point of view.

We are probably all a little cranky in our ideas on manuring. The young man who used to collect the contents from his friends' ashtrays for later application to his roses is a case in point. Tea leaves get saved exclusively as a mulch for camellias, simply because the tea plant is a camellia species. For my part, I cast all my nail parings out of the bathroom window so as to feed the ceanothus below with hoof-and-horn. Since, at twenty-four years, this is the oldest ceanothus in my garden, and it is still flourishing, I naturally congratulate myself on a sagacious policy.

CHRISTOPHER LLOYD,
The Well-Tempered Garden, 1970

Cyril Connolly, sending a book to his gardening friend, Lady Glenconner, in 1953, added a new beatitude to his inscription.

Blessed are the botanists, for they shall inherit a rich fibrous loam.

CYRIL CONNOLLY,
1953

Tennyson was only twenty-one when he wrote this poem, which reveals not the slightest feeling for gardening. (That came later.) The delicious smell of rotting leaves, the garden's finest food, made him feel faint and sick.

The air is damp, and hush'd, and close,
As a sick man's room when he taketh repose
   An hour before death;
My very heart faints and my whole soul grieves
At the moist rich smell of the rotting leaves,
   And the breath
   Of the fading edges of box beneath,
And the year's last rose.
   Heavily hangs the broad sunflower
     Over its grave i' the earth so chilly;
   Heavily hangs the hollyhock,
     Heavily hangs the tiger-lily.

ALFRED LORD TENNYSON,
Songs and Occasional Pieces, 1830

Garden visiting, today a national recreation, is by no means new. It has always been possible to see important houses and gardens by free ticket or payment, or simply by sending in one's card, when the housekeeper or gardener would show the tourist round. Boswell, of course, took the opportunity on such a visit of showing off, and equally of course was put down by Dr Johnson.

On Monday June 4th we all went to Luton Hoo, to see Lord Bute's magnificent seat, for which I had obtained a ticket. As we entered the park, I talked in a high style of my old friendship with Lord Mountstuart, and said, 'I shall probably be much in this place.' The Sage, aware of human vicissitudes, gently checked me: 'Don't you be too sure of that.' He made two or three peculiar observations; as when shown the botanical gardens, 'Is not every garden a botanical garden?' When told there was a shrubbery to the extent of several miles: 'That is making a very foolish use of the ground; a little of it is very well.' When it was proposed that we should walk on the pleasure-ground, 'Don't let us fatigue ourselves. Why should we walk there? Here's a fine tree, let's get to the top of it.' But upon the whole he was very much pleased.

JAMES BOSWELL,
Life of Johnson, 1781

John Evelyn was a dedicated garden visitor, on the continent as well as at home. His descriptions of gardens were rather dull, like an official guidebook.

From hence about a league farther we went to see Cardinal Richelieu's villa at Ruell . . . though the house is not of the greatest, the gardens about it are so magnificent that I doubt whether Italy has any exceeding it for all rarities of pleasure. The garden nearest the pavilion is a parterre, having in the middst divers noble brasse statues, perpetually spouting water into an ample bassin, . . .; but what is most admirable is the vast enclosure, and variety of ground, in the large garden, containing vineyards, cornefields, meadows, groves (whereof one is of perennial greenes), and walkes of vast lengthes, so accurately kept and cultivated, that nothing can be more agreeable . . . This leads to the Citroniere, which is a noble conserve of all those rarities; and at the end of it is the Arch of Constantine, painted on a wall in oyle, as large as the real one at Rome, so well don that even a man skill'd in painting may mistake it for stone and sculpture. The skie and hills which seem to be between the arches are so naturall that swallows and other birds, thinking to fly through, have dashed themselves against the wall. I was infinitely taken with this agreeable cheate.

JOHN EVELYN,
Diary, 1644

Pepys was a regular garden visitor, sometimes by appointment, sometimes dropping in in the course of a long journey, and thoroughly enjoyed such outings.

I come to Hatfield before twelve o'clock, and walked all alone to the Vineyard, which is now a very beautiful place again; and coming back I met with Mr Looker, my Lord's gardener . . . who showed me the house, the chapel with brave pictures, and, above all, the gardens, such as I never saw in all my life; nor so good flowers, nor so great gooseberries, as big as nutmegs.

(1661)

[Lord Brooke's] gardens are excellent; and here I first saw oranges grow: some green, some half, some a quarter, and some full ripe, on the same tree . . . I pulled off a little one by stealth . . . and eat it. Here were also great variety of other exotic plants, and several labyrinths, and a pretty aviary. So in the cool of the evening home.

(1666)

However, I am afraid that Pepys was not an over-conscientious visitor, and today the National Trust would dread him. He allowed children in his party to pick the flowers, and, on other occasions, he helped himself to apples and oranges.

Thence home, and with my wife and the two maids and the boy took boat and to Vauxhall, where I had not been a great while. To the old Spring Garden, and there walked long, and the wenches gathered pinks . . . Thence to the new one, where I never was before, and the boy crept through the hedge and gathered abundance of roses.

(1662)

SAMUEL PEPYS,
Diary

For Elizabeth Bennet, a tourist's visit to Pemberley House, the Derbyshire seat of Mr Darcy, was an occasion of acute embarrassment. Mr Darcy, with whom she was on icy terms, was thought to be away, but he arrived home unexpectedly.

When all the house that was open to general inspection had been seen, they returned down stairs, and taking leave of the housekeeper, were consigned over to the gardener, who met them at the hall door.

As they walked across the lawn towards the river, Elizabeth turned to look back again; her uncle and aunt stopped also, and while the former was conjecturing as to the date of the building, the owner of it himself suddenly came forward from the road, which led behind it to the stables.

They were within twenty yards of each other, and so abrupt was his appearance, that it was impossible to avoid his sight. Their eyes instantly met, and the cheeks of each were overspread with the deepest blush.

JANE AUSTEN,
Pride and Prejudice, 1813

Maud was criticized for its morbidity when it first appeared, and has been accused ever since of a falsity of feeling. I think it is presumptuous to try to judge whether another's love is fancied or real, and the words are wonderful.

Written when Tennyson was in his forties, it looks back to a time when he was unhappily in love with Rosa Baring, a rich young lady who was staying at the fine Caroline mansion, Harrington Hall, in Lincolnshire, a few miles from Somersby Rectory, where Tennyson was born.

A million emeralds break from the ruby-budded lime
In the little grove where I sit — ah, wherefore cannot I be
Like things of the season gay, like the bountiful season bland,
When the far-off sail is blown by the breeze of a softer clime,
Half-lost in the liquid azure bloom of a crescent of sea,
The silent sapphire-spangled marriage ring of the land?

     * * *

  Come into the garden, Maud,
   For the black bat, night, has flown,
  Come into the garden, Maud.
   I am here at the gate alone;
  And the woodbine spices are wafted abroad,
   And the musk of the rose is blown.

  For a breeze of morning moves,
   And the planet of Love is on high,
  Beginning to faint in the light that she loves
   On a bed of daffodil sky,
  To faint in the light of the sun she loves,
   To faint in his light, and to die.

  All night have the roses heard
   The flute, violin, bassoon;
  All night has the casement jessamine stirr'd
   To the dancers dancing in tune;

Till a silence fell with the waking bird,
   And a hush with the setting moon.

I said to the lily, 'There is but one
   With whom she has heart to be gay.
When will the dancers leave her alone?
   She is weary of dance and play.'
Now half to the setting moon are gone,
   And half to the rising day;
Low on the sand and loud on the stone
   The last wheel echoes away.

ALFRED LORD TENNYSON,
Maud, 1855

Now this really is effete. It is Wilfrid Scawen Blunt's idea of heaven.

. . . to be laid out to sleep in a garden, with running water near, and so to sleep for a hundred thousand years, then to be woke by a bird singing, and to call out to the person one loved best, 'Are you there?' and for her to answer, 'Yes, are you?' and so turn round and go to sleep again for another hundred thousand years.

WILFRID SCAWEN BLUNT,
My Diaries, 1897

Swinburne contributes to the melancholy mood.

In a coign of the cliff between lowland and highland,
  At the sea-down's edge between windward and lee,
Walled round with rocks as an inland island,
  The ghost of a garden fronts the sea.
A girdle of brushwood and thorn encloses
  The steep square slope of the blossomless bed
Where the weeds that grew green from the graves of its roses
      Now lie dead.

ALGERNON SWINBURNE,
A Forsaken Garden, 1878

*William Robinson did not invent the wild garden, which had been loved,
especially in England, for hundreds of years. But the Victorian passion for
greenhouses and carpet bedding, billiard-table lawns and cheap statues, had
scarred our country with some of the ugliest gardens ever made, and it was
the fiery William Robinson who sent forth the loudest clarion call demanding
a return to natural, permanent planting. In 1870 he created a stir with*
The Wild Garden, *followed in 1883 by* The English Flower Garden.
In the former book he explains what wild gardening means.

There has been some misunderstanding as to the term 'Wild Garden'.
It is applied essentially to the placing of perfectly hardy exotic plants
under conditions where they will thrive without further care. It has
nothing to do with the old idea of the 'Wilderness'. It does not mean
the picturesque garden, for a garden may be highly picturesque, and
yet in every part the result of ceaseless care.

What it does mean is best explained by the winter Aconite
flowering under a grove of naked trees in February; by the Snowflake,
tall and numerous in meadows by the Thames side; by the blue
Lupine dyeing an islet with its purple in a Scotch river; and by the
blue Apennine Anemone staining an English wood blue before the
coming of our blue bells. Multiply these instances a thousandfold,
given by many types of plants, from countries colder than ours, and
one may get a just idea of the 'Wild Garden'.

WILLIAM ROBINSON,
The Wild Garden (1870), 1894 edition

Robinson's friend and colleague, Miss Jekyll, had been a painter until, in middle age, failing eyesight made her turn her creative talents to professional gardening, and she saw gardens always as a painter. Every garden she designed was to be a picture, or a series of pictures.

Ever since it came to me to feel some grasp of knowledge of means and methods, I have found that my greatest pleasure, both in garden and woodland, has been in the enjoyment of beauty of a pictorial kind. Whether the picture be large as of a whole landscape, or of lesser extent as in some fine single group or effect, or within the space of only a few inches as may be seen in some happily-disposed planting of Alpines, the intention is always the same; or whether it is the grouping of trees in the wood by the removal of those whose lines are not wanted in the picture, or in the laying out of broad grassy ways in woody places, or by ever so slight a turn or change of direction in a wood path, or in the alteration of some arrangement of related groups for form or for massing of light and shade, or for any of the many local conditions that guide one towards forming a decision, the intention is still always the same — to try and make a beautiful garden-picture.

GERTRUDE JEKYLL,
Wood and Garden, 1899

Mr Bowles was a gardener of quite a different school, a collector and plantsman who cultivated the finest forms of plants to perfection. Dare one suggest that Mr Bowles was thinking here of Miss Jekyll and her colour schemes?

I fear I am a little impatient of the school of gardening that encourages the selection of plants merely as artistic furniture, chosen for colour only, like ribbons or embroidery silks. I feel sorry for plants that are obliged to make a struggle for life in uncongenial situations because their owner wishes all things of those shades of pink, blue or orange to fit in next to the grey or crimson planting.

E. A. BOWLES,
My Garden in Spring, 1914

Mrs Earle damned Miss Jekyll with faint praise, and was wonderfully patronizing about her garden at Munstead Wood. But to be fair, there is very little in Miss Jekyll's writings which Mrs Earle had not said before her. Pot-Pourri is one of the best of all gardeners' testaments, a worthy forerunner of E. A. Bowles.

There has been in this year's 'Guardian' a succession of monthly papers on a Surrey garden, written by Miss Jekyll of Munstead Wood, Godalming. I give her address, as she now sells her surplus plants, all more or less suited to light soils, to the management of which she has for many years past given special attention. These papers have much illuminating matter in them, and are called 'Notes from Garden and Woodland'. All the plants and flowers about which Miss Jekyll writes she actually grows on the top of her Surrey hill. Her garden is a most instructive one, and encouraging too. She has gone through the stage, so common to all ambitious and enthusiastic amateurs, of trying to grow everything, and of often wasting much precious room in growing inferior plants, or plants which, even though they may be worth growing in themselves, are not yet worth the care and feeding which a light soil necessitates if they are to be successful.

MRS C. W. EARLE,
Pot-Pourri from a Surrey Garden, 1897

*This beautiful poem is tragically relevant today. Thinking of my own felled
elms — more than thirty of them — I read it often.*

The poplars are fell'd, farewell to the shade
And the whispering sound of the cool colonnade,
The winds play no longer, and sing in the leaves,
Nor Ouse on his bosom their image receives.

Twelve years have elaps'd since I first took a view
Of my favourite field and the bank where they grew,
And now in the grass behold they are laid,
And the tree is my seat that once lent me a shade.

The blackbird has fled to another retreat
Where the hazels afford him a screen from the heat,
And the scene where his melody charm'd me before,
Resounds with his sweet-flowing ditty no more.

WILLIAM COWPER,
The Poplar Field, written after 1786

*There is a great deal of splendid literature on vegetables. In prose and verse,
lyrical, didactic or polemic, gardeners have plunged into the subject with
enthusiasm. Addison was one who rejoiced at the sight of vegetable gardens
which were soon, under the patrons of the picturesque, to be banished far
from the house.*

My kitchen has likewise its particular quarters assigned it; for besides
the wholesome luxury which that place abounds with, I have always
thought a kitchen-garden a more pleasant sight than the finest
orangerie, or artificial green-house. I love to see every thing in its
perfection, and am more pleased to survey my rows of coleworts and
cabbages, with a thousand nameless pot-herbs, springing up in their
full fragrance and verdure, than to see tender plants of foreign
countries kept alive by artificial heats.

JOSEPH ADDISON,
Letter to the *Spectator*, 1712

James Hervey perhaps piled it on a bit too thick.

THE KITCHEN GARDEN

What a fund of choice accommodation is here! what a source of wholesome dainties! and all for the enjoyment of man. Why does the parsley, with her frizzled locks, shag the border; or why the celery, with her whitening arms, perforate the mould; but to render his soups savoury? The asparagus shoots its tapering stems, to offer him the first fruits of the season; and the artichoke spreads its turgid top, to give him a treat of vegetable marrow.

JAMES HERVEY,
Reflections in a Flower Garden, 1746–7

William Cobbett was of the same opinion as Addison. Sensible, irascible, practical, with a passion for the realities of rural life, he preached that the kitchen-garden must be near the house.

It is most miserable taste to seek to poke away the kitchen-garden, in order to get it out of sight. If well managed, nothing is more beautiful than the kitchen-garden: the earliest blossoms come there: we shall in vain seek for flowering shrubs in March, and early in April, to equal the peaches, nectarines, apricots, and plums; late in April, we shall find nothing to equal the pear and the cherry; and, in May, the dwarf, or espalier, apple-trees, are just so many immense garlands of carnations. The walks are unshaded: they are not greasy or covered with moss, in the spring of the year, like those in the shrubberies: to watch the progress of the crops is by no means unentertaining to any rational creature; and the kitchen-garden gives you all this long before the ornamental part of the garden affords you anything worth looking at. Therefore, I see no reason for placing the kitchen-garden in some out-of-the-way place, at a distance from the mansion-house, as if it were a mere necessary evil, and unworthy of being viewed by the owner. In the time of fruiting, where shall we find anything much more beautiful to behold than a tree loaded with cherries, peaches, or apricots, but particularly the two latter? It is curious enough, that people decorate their chimney-pieces with imitations of these beautiful fruits, while they seem to think nothing at all of the originals hanging upon the tree, with all the elegant accompaniments of flourishing branches, buds, and leaves.

WILLIAM COBBETT,
The English Gardener, 1829

Cowper felt that vegetables had not received their meed of praise, and corrects the balance in his long didactic poem, The Task.

> To raise the prickly and green-coated gourd,
> So grateful to the palate, and when rare
> So coveted, else base and disesteem'd —
> Food for the vulgar merely — is an art
> That toiling ages have but just matur'd,
> And at this moment unassay'd in song.
> Yet gnats have had, and frogs and mice, long since,
> Their eulogy; those sang the Mantuan bard,
> And these the Grecian, in ennobling strains;
> And in thy numbers, Phillips, shines for aye
> The solitary shilling. Pardon, then,
> Ye sage dispensers of poetic fame,
> Th'ambition of one, meaner far, whose pow'rs,
> Presuming an attempt not less sublime,
> Pant for the praise of dressing to the taste
> Of critic appetite, no sordid fare,
> A cucumber, while costly yet and scarce.

WILLIAM COWPER,
The Task, 1784

Ambrose Bierce, American satirist and pioneer newspaper columnist, was witty about cabbages.

Cabbage. A familiar kitchen-garden vegetable about as large and wise as a man's head.

AMBROSE BIERCE,
The Enlarged Devil's Dictionary, 1906

One of the most extravagant cookery books ever written is The Alice B. Toklas Cook Book, *by the lifelong friend of Gertrude Stein. So elaborate are its recipes that I have never managed to cook a single one.*

These two American ladies lived for literature, friends and food, not necessarily in that order. They spent most of their lives in France and Miss Stein grew mountainously fat, and even Miss Toklas, who was in charge of the vegetable gardens at their home at Bilignin, near the French Alps, where they lived in the nineteen-thirties, found it difficult to weed and gather from the narrow paths. Miss Toklas also supervised the cooking, which was on a magnificent scale, and waited on Miss Stein hand and foot — she was content to spend an hour picking alpine strawberries in the garden for Miss Stein's breakfast.

If the book is not exactly a vade mecum *for the family cook, it is delightful to read for the procession of personalities who ate at Miss Stein's table and entertained the two ladies in return, princesses and artists, writers and maîtres d'hotel, English milords and visiting Americans. There is a secondary procession, equally interesting, of the French domestics who served this hospitable household, few of whom had the stamina to stay for long.*

The vegetable gardens at Bilignin were stocked with a wide range of gourmet vegetables grown from seed obtained from many regions, including gumbo from the south of France and sweet corn from the United States. Almost all one needs to know about growing and cooking vegetables is summed up in these three paragraphs.

The first gathering of the garden in May of salads, radishes and herbs made me feel like a mother about her baby — how could anything so beautiful be mine. And this emotion of wonder filled me for each vegetable as it was gathered every year. There is nothing that is comparable to it, as satisfactory or as thrilling, as gathering the vegetables one has grown.

Later when the vegetables were ready to be picked it never occurred to us to question what way to cook them. Naturally the simplest, just to steam or boil them and serve them with the excellent country butter or cream that we had from a farmer almost within calling distance. Later still, when we had guests and the vegetables had lost the aura of a new-born miracle, sauces added variety.

In the beginning it was the habit to pick all vegetables very young except beetroots, potatoes and large squash and pumpkins because of one's eagerness, and later because of their delicate flavour when cooked. That prevented serving sauces with some vegetables – green peas, string beans (indeed all peas and beans) and lettuces, but there were exceptions.

The Alice B. Toklas Cook Book, 1954

Unlike Miss Toklas, Professor Carey cannot bear his vegetables to be eaten. He has something in common with the mad art collector who gloats over his stolen masterpieces in the cellar and shares them with no other eyes. He wants to grow exquisite vegetables as an aesthetic experience, and perish the thought that they should be eaten. What, one wonders, is his wife allowed to cook for Sunday lunch?

As vegetable gardeners aren't primarily concerned with eating they harbour, like librarians, a tidy-minded dislike of anyone who actually wants to use the commodities they're in charge of. To have to uproot cabbages, say, from a row, and hand them over for cooking, is always an annoyance. The gaps look unsightly, like snapped-off teeth. A stalwart, unbroken line of cabbages, on the other hand, with their hearts tight as fists and their purple outer leaves spread to catch the dew, raise your spirit every time you visit them. Among the current clichés I especially deplore is the one which refers to hospital patients kept alive by machines as 'cabbages'. This is both inaccurate and insulting to vegetables. For a cabbage is a sturdy, self-reliant being, and compared with an average specimen of twentieth-century manhood it has, when well grown, a positively athletic air.

PROFESSOR JOHN CAREY,
The Sunday Times, 1980

Lest you should think vegetable growing is child's play, there is Dr Hessayon to put you right.

Greenhouse cucumbers are a delicate crop, and a host of bacterial and fungal infections can attack them. Most of these arise through incorrect soil preparation or careless management of the growing plants . . . Outdoor cucumbers and marrows are much simpler to grow and are generally trouble-free, although slugs, grey mould, powdery mildew and cucumber mosaic virus can cause serious losses.

DR D. G. HESSAYON,
Be Your Own Vegetable Doctor, 1978

Today I find Kipling, a favourite author of my childhood, very hard to take, and this celebrated poem is unendurably edifying. But I print three verses as a significant period piece.

There's not a pair of legs so thin, there's not a head so thick,
There's not a hand so weak and white, nor yet a heart so sick,
But it can find some needful job that's crying to be done,
For the Glory of the Garden glorifieth every one.

Then seek your job with thankfulness and work till further
orders,
If it's only netting strawberries or killing slugs on borders;
And when your back stops aching and your hands begin to
harden,
You will find yourself a partner in the Glory of the Garden.

Oh, Adam was a gardener, and God who made him sees
That half a proper gardener's work is done upon his knees,
So when your work is finished, you can wash your hands and
pray
For the Glory of the Garden that it may not pass away!
And the Glory of the Garden it shall never pass away!

RUDYARD KIPLING,
The Glory of the Garden, 1911

One of the greatest men in the history of gardening was John Claudius Loudon, gardener, planner, traveller, reformer, teacher, and encyclopaedic writer, all of whose works have given me pleasure. But they are too closely argued and informative to 'cut' well, and I am leaving it to his gifted and devoted wife Jane, a heroine in her own right, to pay him tribute. She tells of his childhood:

At this early period . . . a taste for landscape-gardening began to show itself, as his principal pleasure was in making walks and beds in a little garden his father had given him; and so eager was he to obtain seeds to sow in it, that, when a jar of tamarinds arrived from an uncle in the West Indies, he gave the other children his share of the fruit, on condition of his having all the *seeds*.

And later in the same biography:

Mr Loudon reached St Petersburgh on the 30th of October, just before the breaking up of the bridge, and he remained there three or four months; after which he proceeded to Moscow, where he arrived on the 4th of March, 1814, after having encountered various difficulties on the road. Once, in particular, the horses in his carriage being unable to drag it through a snowdrift, the postilions very coolly unharnessed them and trotted off, telling him that they would bring fresh horses in the morning, and that he would be in no danger from the wolves if he would keep the windows of his carriage close, and the leather curtains down. There was no remedy but to submit; and few men were better fitted by nature for bearing the horrors of such a night than Mr Loudon, from his natural calmness and patient endurance of difficulties. He often, however, spoke of the situation he was in, particularly when he heard the howling of the wolves, and once when a herd of them rushed across the road close to his carriage. He had also some doubts whether the postilions would be able to recollect where they had left the carriage, as the wind had been very high during the night, and had blown the snow through the crevices in the curtains. The morning, however, brought the postilions with fresh horses, and the remainder of the journey was passed without any difficulty.

JANE LOUDON,
A Short Account of the Life and Writings of John Claudius Loudon, 1845

My husband and I once rented an old house in Greece for the month of
August, and the owner left us lengthy instructions for watering the garden
in his absence. 'You will find the zinnias particularly rewarding.' However,
we were delighted to find on going round the garden that all the flowers were
already quite dead, especially as the water had to be hauled up by bucket
from a well. We were luckier than Karel Čapek's persecuted friend.

August usually is the time when the amateur gardener forsakes his
garden of wonder and goes on leave. The whole year long he vehemently
swore that this year he would not go anywhere, that a garden is worth
more than all summer resorts, and that he, the gardener, was not such
a fool and ass as to be harassed by trains and all the devils; nevertheless,
when summer sets in even he deserts the town, either because the
nomadic instinct has awakened in him or to keep his neighbours from
talking. He departs, however, with a heavy heart, full of fears and cares
for his garden; and he will not go until he has found a friend or relation
to whom he entrusts his garden for that time.

'Look here,' he says, 'there is nothing to be done now in the
garden in any case; if you come and look once in three days, that will
be quite enough, and if something here and there is not in order, you
must write me a card, and I will come. So, I am relying on you then?
As I said, five minutes will be enough, just a glance round.'

Then he leaves, having laid his garden upon the heart of an
obliging fellow-creature. Next day the fellow-creature receives a
letter: 'I forgot to tell you that the garden must be watered every
day, the best times for doing it are five in the morning and towards
seven in the evening. It is practically nothing, you only fasten the
hose to the hydrant and water for a few moments. Will you please
water the conifers all over as they stand, and thoroughly, and the
lawn as well? If you see any weeds, pull them out. That's all.'

A day after: 'It is frightfully dry, will you give every rhododendron
about two buckets of tepid water, and each conifer five buckets, and
other trees about four buckets? The perennials, which are now in

flower, ought to have a good deal of water — write by return post what is in flower. Withered stalks must be cut off! It would be a good thing if you loosened all the beds with a hoe; the soil breathes much better then. If there are plant-lice on the roses, buy tobacco extract, and syringe them with it while the dew is on, or after a rain. Nothing else need be done at present.'

The third day: 'I forgot to tell you that the lawn must be cut; you can do it easily with the mower, and what the mower does not take, you cut with clippers. But beware! after mowing the grass it must be well raked, and afterwards *swept with a sweeper*! Otherwise the lawn gets bald patches! And water, plenty of water!'

The fourth day: 'If a storm comes, will you please run and look at my garden? A heavy rain sometimes causes damage, and it is good to be on the spot. If mildew appears on the roses, sprinkle them early in the morning while the dew is still on them with flowers of sulphur. Tie high perennials to sticks so that the wind does not break them. It is glorious here, mushrooms are growing and the swimming is beautiful. Don't forget to water every day the ampelopsis near the house, it is too dry for it there. Keep for me in a packet the seeds of *Papaver nudicaule*. I hope that you have already mown the lawns. You needn't do anything else, but destroy earwigs.'

The fifth day: 'I am sending you a box of plants, which I dug up here in a wood. They are various orchids, wild lilies, Pasque flowers, pirolas, bugworts, anemones, and others. Immediately you have got the box, open it, and damp the seedlings, and plant them somewhere in a shady place! Add peat and leafmould! Plant immediately and water three times a day! Please cut the side branches of the roses.'

The sixth day: 'I am sending you by express post a box of plants from the country . . . They must go into the ground at once . . . At night you ought to go into the garden with a lamp and destroy snails. It would be good to weed the paths. I hope that looking after my garden doesn't take up much of your time, and that you are enjoying it.'

KAREL ČAPEK,
The Gardener's Year, 1931

Domicilium is Thomas Hardy's earliest known poem, written between 1857 and 1860, 'a prototypical Hardy poem: local to himself', in the words of his anthologist, David Wright. It is a description of the cottage in Dorset where he was born in 1840 (now happily in the hands of the National Trust), the starting-point for the Wessex novels and poems.

It faces west, and round the back and sides
High beeches, bending, hang a veil of boughs,
And sweep against the roof. Wild honeysucks
Climb on the walls, and seem to sprout a wish
(If we may fancy wish of trees and plants)
To overtop the apple-trees hard by.

Red Roses, lilacs, variegated box
Are there in plenty, and such hardy flowers
As flourish best untrained. Adjoining these
Are herbs and esculents; and farther still
A field; then cottages with trees, and last
The distant hills and sky.

THOMAS HARDY,
Domicilium

Babies are a kind of crop in a slummy garden in Wales.

Me, Polly Garter, under the washing line, giving the breast in the garden to my bonny new baby. Nothing grows in our garden, only washing. And babies. And where's their fathers live, my love? Over the hills and far away . . . Oh, isn't life a terrible thing, thank God!

DYLAN THOMAS,
Under Milk Wood, first performed 1952

Babies and plants are weirdly interwoven in this lady gardener's mind.

Since the birth of our son the garden's been neglected, but weeds aren't the only things that have flourished. The other evening, I found seedlings of variegated lamium, cotoneaster, hypericum, hollyhock, a germinated orange pip and some very interesting unknowns. So we have increased our stock in more ways than one.

Letter to a gardening magazine, 1982

To generalize about gardening leads one into awful traps. We think of the French, rightly for the most part, as formal gardeners with a genius for the culture of trees. Personally, I like to see trees superlatively pleached or pruned, but Horace Walpole, a man for clumps, thought the French were tree torturers.

. . . As your particular friend, [I] will communicate a rare improvement on nature, which these great philosophers have made . . . It is nothing but this: trees ought to be educated as much as men, and are strange awkward productions when not taught to hold themselves upright or bow on proper occasions. The academy *de belles-lettres* have even offered a prize for the man that shall recover the long-lost art of an ancient Greek, called *le sieur Orphée*, who instituted a dancing-school for plants, and gave a magnificent ball on the birth of the Dauphin of Thrace, which was performed entirely by forest-trees. In this whole kingdom there is no such thing as seeing a tree that is not well-behaved. They are first stripped up and then cut down; and you would as soon meet a man with his hair about his ears as an oak or an ash. As the weather is very hot now, and the soil chalk, and the dust white, I assure you it is very difficult, powdered as both are all over, to distinguish a tree from a hair-dresser. Lest this should sound like a travelling hyperbole, I must advertise your Lordship, that there is little difference in their heights; for, a tree of thirty years' growth being liable to be marked as royal timber, the proprietors take care not to let their trees live to the age of being enlisted, but burn them, and plant others as often almost as they change their fashions. This gives an air of perpetual youth to the face of the country.

HORACE WALPOLE
to the Earl of Strafford,
from Paris, 1769, *Letters*, Vol. V

Only nine years before Walpole was condemning French gardeners as incurable snippers, Rousseau was writing of one of the wildest wild gardens ever imagined. In his slightly absurd novel, Julie: ou La Nouvelle Hélöise, *Julie has a woodland garden, which she called her elysium, where the gardener worked for but twelve days a year. Garden plants were naturalized along with wild plants, and Julie encouraged throngs of birds, and scattered hair, straw, wool and moss for their nests in spring. A friend describes this secret garden.*

Upon entering this disguised orchard, I was seized with an agreeable sensation; the freshness of the thick foliage, the beautiful and lovely verdure, the flowers scattered on each side, the murmuring of the purling stream and the warbling of a thousand birds, struck my imagination as powerfully as my senses; but at the same time I thought myself in the most wild and solitary place in nature, and I appeared as if I had been the first mortal who had ever penetrated into this desart spot . . .

I began to wander over the orchard thus metamorphosed with a kind of ecstasy; and if I found no exotic plants, nor any of the products of the Indies, I found all those which were natural to the soil, disposed and blended in such a manner as to produce the most cheerful and lively effect. The verdant turf, thick, but short and close, was intermixed with wild thyme, balm, sweet marjoram, and other fragrant herbs. You might perceive a thousand wild flowers dazzle your eyes, among which you would be surprised to discover some garden-flowers, which seemed to grow natural with the rest. I now and then met with shady tufts as impervious to the rays of the sun, as if they had been in a thick forest. These tufts were composed of trees of a very flexible nature, the branches of which they bend till they hang on the ground, and take root, as I have seen some trees naturally do in America. In the more open spots, I saw here and there bushes of roses, raspberries, and gooseberries, little plantations of lilac, hazle-trees, alders, seringa, broom, and trefoil, dispersed without any order or symmetry, and which embellished the ground, at the same time that it gave the appearance of being overgrown with weeds. I followed the track through irregular and serpentine walks, bordered by these flowery thickets, and covered with a thousand garlands composed of vines, hops, rose-weed, snake-weed, and other plants of that kind, with which honeysuckles and jessamine deigned to intertwine! . . .

The groves on this side served as an asylum to that vast number of birds which I had heard chirping at a distance; and it was under the shade of their foliage, as under a large umbrella, that you might see them hop about, run, frisk, provoke each other, and fight, as if they had not perceived us.

JEAN-JACQUES ROUSSEAU,
Julie: ou La Nouvelle Hélöise, 1760

A Frenchman of our own time, André Gide, also liked a certain informality in the garden, but he had the Frenchman's traditional appreciation of trees, and cultivated them to a high standard.

Radiant weather since yesterday. Wonderfully limpid sky. For the first time I went out of the garden . . . and went down to the valley . . . The brush is being cut on the hill; the landscape seems enlarged by this; the tall trees that have been left seem more graceful, more noble. A slight vapour gave distance to the various planes so that I hardly recognized this valley, and surprise was mingled with my delight . . .

I have done nothing almost all day long, filled as I was with admiration; it entered through every sense.

I worked at length on the trees; having asked Valentine to lime the trunks of those in the hothouse garden, I noticed that it would be wise to brush the trunks first. In the toolshed I discovered a brush with metal bristles and went at the job zealously. I cleaned off an unbelievable amount of moss, lichen, and dust, and the trunks of the young trees appeared smooth, shining, soft in colour, and pleasant to the touch and to the eye. They looked like handsome naked athletes rubbed with oil, stalwart, and with muscles taut.

I am struck with wonder . . . by the beauty of bark; and what a difference, from one tree to another, in grain, tone, and quality!

ANDRÉ GIDE,
Journal, year 1916

Some gardens are positively sinister. Alice saw one in her dream.

A large rose-tree stood near the entrance of the garden: the roses growing on it were white, but there were three gardeners at it, busily painting them red. Alice thought this a very curious thing, and she went nearer to watch them, and, just as she came up to them, she heard one of them say 'Look out now, Five! Don't go splashing paint over me like that!'

'I couldn't help it,' said Five, in a sulky tone. 'Seven jogged my elbow.'

On which Seven looked up and said 'That's right, Five! Always lay the blame on others!'

'*You'd* better not talk!' said Five. 'I heard the Queen say only yesterday you deserved to be beheaded.'

'What for?' said the one who had spoken first.

'That's none of *your* business, Two!' said Seven.

'Yes, it *is* his business!' said Five. 'And I'll tell him — it was for bringing the cook tulip-roots instead of onions.'

LEWIS CARROLL,
Alice's Adventures in Wonderland, 1865

Hardy, always preoccupied with tombs and death, saw ghosts in the garden.

Its former green is blue and thin,
And its once firm legs sink in and in;
Soon it will break down unaware,
Soon it will break down unaware.

At night when reddest flowers are black
Those who once sat thereon come back;
Quite a row of them sitting there,
Quite a row of them sitting there.

With them the seat does not break down,
Nor winter freeze them, nor floods drown,
For they are light as upper air,
They are light as upper air.

THOMAS HARDY,
The Garden Seat

Donne reflected on the mortality of flowers.

Little think'st thou, poore flower,
Whom I have watchd sixe or seaven dayes,
And seene thy birth, and seene what every houre
Gave to thy growth, thee to this height to raise,
And now dost laugh and triumph on this bough,
      Little think'st thou
That it will freeze anon, and that I shall
To morrow finde thee falne, or not at all.

JOHN DONNE,
The Blossom

Frances Hodgson Burnett created a disturbing world of morbid memories and sickly children. A Yorkshire squire, Mr Craven, lost his wife in giving birth to a son, Colin, who has been brought up a pampered invalid, believing that he will grow a hump and die young. But he is cured by playing with other children in a garden. This is a favourite book with many of my women friends, but not with me.

'Everyone is obliged to do what pleases me,' [Colin] said indifferently. 'It makes me ill to be angry. No one believes I shall live to grow up . . . How old are you?' he asked.

'I am ten,' answered Mary, '. . . and so are you.'

'How do you know that?' he demanded in a surprised voice.

'Because when you were born the garden door was locked and the key was buried. And it has been locked for ten years.'

Colin half sat up, turning toward her, leaning on his elbows.

'What garden door was locked? Who did it? Where was the key buried?' . . .

'It – it was the garden Mr Craven hates,' said Mary nervously. 'He locked the door. No one – no one knew where he buried the key.'

FRANCES HODGSON BURNETT,
The Secret Garden, 1911

It is quite a relief to turn to the cheerful cuttiness of Nancy Mitford.

Planes was a horrible house. It was an overgrown cottage, that is to say, the rooms were large, with all the disadvantages of a cottage, low ceilings, small windows with diamond panes, uneven floorboards, and a great deal of naked knotted wood. It was furnished neither in good nor bad taste, but simply with no attempt at taste at all, and was not even very comfortable. The garden which lay around it would be a lady water-colourist's heaven, herbaceous borders, rockeries, and water-gardens were carried to a perfection of vulgarity, and flaunted a riot of huge and hideous flowers, each individual bloom appearing twice as large, three times as brilliant as it ought to have been and if possible of a different colour from that which nature intended. It would be hard to say whether it was more frightful, more like glorious Technicolor, in spring, in summer, or in autumn. Only in the depth of winter, covered by the kindly snow, did it melt into the landscape and become tolerable . . .

We motored down past acres of blossom.

'The great difference,' said Linda, 'between Surrey and proper, real country, is that in Surrey, when you see blossom, you know there will be no fruit. Think of the Vale of Evesham, and then look at all this pointless pink stuff — it gives you quite a different feeling. The garden at Planes will be a riot of sterility, just you wait.'

It was. You could hardly see any beautiful, pale, bright, yellow-green of spring, every tree appeared to be entirely covered with a waving mass of pink or mauve tissue-paper. The daffodils were so thick on the ground that they too obscured the green, they were new varieties of a terrifying size, either dead white or dark yellow, thick and fleshy; they did not look at all like the fragile friends of one's childhood. The whole effect was of a scene for musical comedy, and it exactly suited Sir Leicester, who, in the country, gave a surprisingly adequate performance of the old English squire.

NANCY MITFORD,
Love in a Cold Climate, 1945

I must say, I would like to have been at this picnic. I am particularly fond of lobster.

'My Lord has ordered the char-a-banc, and is going to drive us all to Chart, where we will lunch,' said Lady St Jerome; ' 'tis a curious place, and was planted only seventy years ago by my Lord's grandfather, entirely with spruce firs, but with so much care and skill, giving each plant and tree ample distance, that they have risen to the noblest proportions, and with all their green branches far-spreading on the ground like huge fans.'

It was only a drive of three or four miles entirely in the park. This was a district that had been added to the ancient enclosure; a striking scene. It was a forest of firs, but quite unlike such as might be met with in the north of Europe or of America. Every tree was perfect, huge and complete, and full of massy grace . . .

They sate down by the great trees, the servants opened the luncheon baskets, which were a present from Balmoral. Lady St Jerome was seldom seen to greater advantage than distributing her viands under such circumstances. Never was such gay and graceful hospitality. Lothair was quite fascinated as she playfully thrust a paper of lobster sandwiches into his hand, and enjoined Monsignore Catesby to fill his tumbler with Chablis.

BENJAMIN DISRAELI,
Lothair, 1870

*Oriental gardens are often a disappointment to vulgar western eyes. In Japan
I have stared and stared at raked sand and symbolic stones without
generating any emotion at all. One has to live there to understand them.
Lafcadio Hearn was an Irishman who went to Tokyo in 1891, married a
Japanese girl, and became a Japanese citizen.*

In order to comprehend the beauty of a Japanese garden, it is
necessary to understand – or at least to learn to understand – the
beauty of stones. Not of stones quarried by the hand of man, but of
stones shaped by nature only. Until you can feel, and keenly feel,
that stones have character, that stones have tones and values, the
whole artistic meaning of a Japanese garden cannot be revealed to
you.

LAFCADIO HEARN,
Glimpses of Unfamiliar Japan, 1894

The diplomatist Algernon Freeman-Mitford also lived in Japan, where he thought the scenery superb, but the gardens ridiculous. He even made an English garden in Tokyo with massed irises which his Japanese friends thought 'only pardonable in a barbarian'. However, on his return to England he made a garden of plants from all over the world, including a large collection of bamboos.

The Japanese are true lovers of scenery; no people have a keener feeling for a beautiful landscape; to them a moon rising over mount Fuji is a poem . . . and yet, strange to say, in their gardens they seem to take a delight in setting at defiance every one of those canons which Nature has laid down so unmistakably for those who will be at the pains to read them. The Japanese garden is a mere toy that might be the appanage of a doll's house. Everything is in miniature.

ALGERNON FREEMAN-MITFORD,
The Bamboo Garden, 1896

Reginald Farrer was another botanist who lived in Japan and fully understood the gardens, but he regretted the exclusiveness of the Japanese taste in flowers.

The Japanese is not the lover of flowers in general that ecstatic British ignorance imagines. A flower, to be admitted by Japanese canons, must conform to certain rigid rules. No flower that fails to do so can be recognized. At the top of rejected blossoms stand the rose and the lily, both of whom are considered by the Japanese rather crude, unrefined efforts of nature.

REGINALD FARRER,
The Garden of Asia, 1904

Persian gardens have also caused disappointment, as Robert Byron discovered in the nineteen-thirties. By then the famous old gardens, cool with trees and water, flowery with fruit blossom, and scented with roses, were in decadence, while under the last two shahs many of the old palaces were pulled down in a frenzy of modernization.

One pollarded tree-stump, an empty pond, and a line of washing all dripping with rain, give a new idea of a Persian garden.

ROBERT BYRON,
The Road to Oxiana, 1937

Elizabeth von Arnim made an English garden, full of roses, bulbs and flowering shrubs, in north Germany. She was married to an insufferable Prussian count referred to throughout this clever, witty book as the Man of Wrath, for he found fault from morning to night. She escaped whenever she could to their remote country house, taking her three little girls with her.

May 16. The garden is the place I go to for refuge and shelter, not the house. In the house are duties and annoyances, servants to exhort and admonish, furniture and meals; but out there blessings crowd round me at every step — it is there that I am sorry for the unkindness in me . . . it is there that all my sins and silliness are forgiven, there that I feel protected and at home, and every flower and weed is a friend and every tree a lover.

January 15 . . . The Man of Wrath does not in the least want roses, or flowering shrubs, or plantations, or new paths, and therefore, he asks, why should he pay for them? . . . By the time the babies have grown old and disagreeable it will be very pretty here, and then possibly they won't like it; and, if they have inherited the Man of Wrath's indifference to gardens, they will let it run wild and leave it to return to the state in which I found it.

ELIZABETH VON ARNIM,
Elizabeth and Her German Garden, 1898

This is one of the garden scenes which has stayed in my memory for many years. Odysseus was most fortunate in his family. Not only was Penelope faithful and Telemachus filial, but his father Laertes laboured to keep up his garden in Ithaca while he was dawdling home from Troy. The moving meeting between father and son after twenty years' absence takes place in the orchard.

He found his father alone in the well-ordered orchard digging round a tree. He was wearing a filthy tunic, patched and shabby, oxhide leggings, also patched, round his legs, to protect them from scratches, and gloves on his hands because of the brambles. On his head was a goatskin cap, and he was nursing his sorrow. When noble, long-suffering Odysseus saw him, wasted with age and with great grief in his heart, he halted under a tall pear-tree and wept. Then he debated in his mind and heart whether to kiss and embrace his father and tell him all, how he had returned to his native land, or whether to question him first and make thorough trial of him. As he pondered, this seemed to him the better way, to test him first with scoffing words, and with this in mind Odysseus went straight to the spot where, with his head down, the old man was hoeing round the tree; and his illustrious son stood beside him and spoke to him.

'Old man, you are not unskilled at tending a garden. Everything is well cared for, and there is not a plant – not a fig, or vine, or olive, or pear – nor a garden-bed in the whole plantation which is not looked after. But I will tell you something else, at which you must not be angry. You yourself are not so well cared for, but carry your years heavily, and you are sadly dirty and poorly dressed . . . But come tell me this truly, whose servant are you, and whose garden do you tend?'

HOMER,
The Odyssey, Book XXIV

Odysseus does not keep Laertes long in doubt. His father tells him of the troubles in Ithaca, and Odysseus reveals himself and tells him that the suitors are slain. The old man is made happy at last.

This is another garden scene which I often go back to. The Semi-Attached Couple *is almost my favourite novel, so enjoyable that I have to ration myself to reading it only once a year. The author, Emily Eden, was the sister of a disastrous governor-general of India, Lord Auckland, for whom she acted as hostess, writing home some charming and perceptive letters.*

The heroine of the novel, Lady Teviot, is newly married to a loving but pathologically jealous lord, and the marriage nearly founders on the honeymoon, where one suspects that the sex has been a failure.

When Lord Teviot had despatched his letters, he found her in her garden; not one of the old-fashioned gardens, full of roses and honeysuckles, and sweet peas, suggestive of the country, and redolent of sweetness — but in a first-rate gardener's garden, every plant forming part of a group, and not to be picked or touched on any account; all of them forced into bloom at the wrong time of the year; and each bearing a name that it was difficult to pronounce, and impossible to remember. Helen was standing apparently absorbed in . admiration of a Lancifolium speciosum, which she had been assured by her gardener was 'a better variety' of the Lancifolium punctatum; but in reality she was thinking first of her mother, wondering when she should see her again; and next what she could find to say to Lord Teviot at dinner.

Helen was joined in the garden by her husband, who almost immediately provoked a row.

EMILY EDEN,
The Semi-Attached Couple, 1830

There are two ways of making gardening a pleasure in winter. One is to have an indoor garden, a warm, bright greenhouse safe from wind and snow.

Who loves a garden loves a greenhouse too.
Unconscious of a less propitious clime,
There blooms exotic beauty, warm and snug,
While the winds whistle, and the snows descend.
The spiry myrtle with unwith'ring leaf
Shines there and flourishes. The golden boast
Of Portugal and western India there,
The ruddier orange, and the paler lime,
Peep through their polish'd foliage at the storm.
And seem to smile at what they need not fear.
Th'amomum there with intermingling flow'rs
And cherries hangs her twigs. Geranium boasts
Her crimson honours, and the spangled beau,
Ficoides, glitters bright the winter long.
All plants, of ev'ry leaf, that can endure
The winter's frown, if screen'd from his shrewd bite,
Live there, and prosper.

WILLIAM COWPER,
The Task, 1784

Another way is to grow plenty of those hardy winter plants which flower bravely outdoors in the darkest months.

> Still may you with your frozen fingers cut
> Treasures of Winter, if you planted well;
> The Winter-sweet against a sheltering wall,
> Waxen, Chinese and drooping bell;
> Strange in its colour, almond in its smell;
> And the Witch-hazel, *Hamamelis mollis*,
> That comes before its leaf on naked bough,
> Torn ribbons frayed, of yellow and maroon,
> And sharp of scent in frosty English air . . .
> Gardener, if you listen, listen well:
> Plant for your winter pleasure, when the months
> Dishearten; plant to find a fragile note
> Touched from the brittle violin of frost.

V. SACKVILLE-WEST,
The Garden, 1946

This charming little book is packed with sensible ideas. Try this one when you are debating whether it is time to sow your sweet peas.

We should not sow when the ground is too cold for the good of the seed, and are less likely to do so if we are told we must be naked when we do it. We have heard that in Lincolnshire, to test whether the soil was in the right condition for sowing barley, farmers used to take off their trousers and sit on the ground: if it was comfortable for them it would be comfortable for the barley.

MAUREEN AND BRIDGET BOLAND,
Old Wives' Lore for Gardeners, 1976

Companion planting is surely more than old wives' lore. It must make scientific sense to plant together things which take different elements from the soil, or even contribute virtues to the soil, as beans do.

DOCTOR FOXGLOVE

Where old cottage gardens still survive, plants that over many years have been found to grow well together will be seen still doing so in what to the suburban-trained eye will seem a terrible muddle. When carriage lamps appear on either side of the cottage door and one of those gardens fit for the ideal home is laid out, among the first things to go on the bonfire (not even the compost heap) are the ordinary old purple foxgloves with which the whole place will have been dotted. Yet the cottager's old wife could have told the newcomers there is nothing to stimulate growth and help disease resistance like the common foxglove. Apart from keeping plants healthier, they will improve the storage qualities of such things as potatoes, tomatoes and apples grown near them.

MAUREEN AND BRIDGET BOLAND
Old Wives' Lore for Gardeners, 1976

If I were to put in this little piece from Peter Rabbit without a provenance
every reader would know it at once, for Beatrix Potter wrote and illustrated
the most memorable books for children (and parents) in the world.

First he ate some lettuces and some French beans; and then he ate
some radishes; and then, feeling rather sick, he went to look for
some parsley.

   But round the end of the cucumber frame, whom should he meet
but Mr McGregor!

BEATRIX POTTER,
The Tale of Peter Rabbit, 1902

*There is a remarkable likeness between Laurie Lee's mother and Colette's
mother, Sido. Was Laurie Lee remembering Colette when he wrote* Cider
with Rosie? *Or do green-fingered mothers tend to beget poetic writers?*

Mother's father had a touch with horses; she had the same with
flowers. She could grow them anywhere, at any time, and they
seemed to live longer for her. She grew them with rough, almost
slap-dash love, but her hands possessed such an understanding of
their needs they seemed to turn to her like another sun. She could
snatch a dry root from field or hedgerow, dab it into the garden, give
it a shake – and almost immediately it flowered. One felt she could
grow roses from a stick or chair-leg, so remarkable was this gift.

Our terrace strip of garden was Mother's monument, and she
worked it headstrong, without plan. She would never control or
clear this ground, merely cherish whatever was there; and she was as
impartial in her encouragement to all that grew as a spell of sweet
sunny weather. She would force nothing, graft nothing, nor set
things in rows; she welcomed self-seeders, let each have its head,
and was the enemy of very few weeds. Consequently our garden was
a sprouting jungle and never an inch was wasted. Syringa shot up,
laburnum hung down, white roses smothered the apple tree, red
flowering-currants (smelling sharply of foxes) spread entirely along
one path; such a chaos of blossom as amazed the bees and bewildered
the birds in the air. Potatoes and cabbages were planted at random
among foxgloves, pansies, and pinks. Often some species would
entirely capture the garden – forget-me-nots one year, hollyhocks
the next, then a sheet of harvest poppies. Whatever it was, one let
it grow. While Mother went creeping around the wilderness, pausing
to tap some odd bloom on the head, as indulgent, gracious, amiable
and inquisitive as a queen at an orphanage.

LAURIE LEE,
Cider with Rosie, 1959

In compiling this book, I have been resisting all the way an inclination to overload it with cottage gardens, for I am particularly fond of them. I hope I may be forgiven for including this longish piece, as it is one of the earliest detailed descriptions of a cottage garden and I find it very moving. The writer is a philanthropist and pamphleteer, but he can tell a tale with the precision of Jane Austen. Most cottage literature tugs at the heartstrings with pictures of poverty and dispossession, but here nearly everybody behaves well.

Two miles from Tadcaster, on the left-hand side of the road to York, stands a beautiful little cottage, with a garden, that has long attracted the eye of the traveller. The slip of land, is exactly a rood, inclosed by a cut quick hedge; and containing the cottage, fifteen apple-trees, one green gage, and three winesour plum-trees, two apricot-trees, several gooseberry and currant bushes, abundance of common vegetables, and three hives of bees; being all the apparent wealth of the possessor . . . In the end of May, 1797, I called there in my way from York; but found the house and the gate of the garden locked. In the road to Tadcaster, however, I met his wife, laden with a basket of provisions from the market; and engaged her to find her husband, who was at work about a mile off, and to send him to me at the inn at Tadcaster. When he arrived he very willingly gave me his history, as follows:

His name is Britton Abbot; his age sixty-seven, and his wife's nearly the same. At nine years old he had gone to work with a farmer; and being a steady careful lad, and a good labourer, particularly in what is called task-work, he had managed so well, that before he was twenty-two years of age, he had accumulated near £.40. He then married, and took a little farm at £.30 a year; but before the end of the second year he found it prudent, or rather necessary, to quit it; having already exhausted, in his attempt to thrive upon it, almost all the little property that he had heaped together. He then fixed in a cottage at Poppleton; where, with two acres of land, and his common right, he kept two cows. Here he had resided very comfortably, as a labourer, for nine years, and had six children living, and his wife preparing to lie in of a seventh, when an inclosure of Poppleton took place; and the arrangements made in consequence of it, obliged him to seek for a new habitation, and other means of subsistence for his family.

He applied to Squire Fairfax, and told him that, if he would let him have a little bit of ground by the road-side, 'he would shew him the *fashions* on it.' After enquiry into his character, he obtained of Mr Fairfax the ground he now occupies; and, with a little assistance from the neighbours, in the carriage of his materials, he built his present house; and planted the garden, and the hedge round it, which is a single row of quick, thirty-five years old, and without a flaw or defect. He says he cut it down six times successively when it was young. Mr Fairfax was so much pleased with the progress of his work, and the extreme neatness of his place, that he told him he should be rent free . . .

He has had seven children; six of whom attained to man's estate; and five are now living, and thriving in the world. One is a carpenter at York; another occupies a little farm at Kelfield; a third is the wife of a labourer, who has built a cottage for himself at Tadcaster, and wants nothing (as the father observed) but a bit of ground for a garden. Britton Abbot says he now earns 12s. and sometimes 15s. and 18s a week, by hoeing turnips by the piece, setting quick, and other task-work: 'but to be sure' (he added) *I have a grand character in all this country.*' He gets from his garden, annually, about forty bushels of potatoes, besides other vegetables; and his fruit is worth from £3 to 4 a year. His wife occasionally goes out to work; she also spins at home, and takes care of his house and garden. He says they have lived very happy together for forty-five years.

THOMAS BERNARD,
An Account of a Cottage Garden near Tadcaster, 1797

Most of the happy descriptions about cottage gardens were written in the south of England. This is Surrey.

A little way to the right (going from London) lies the vile, rotten Borough of Bletchingley; but, happily for Godstone, out of sight. At and near Godstone the gardens are all very neat; and at the Inn there is a nice garden well stocked with beautiful flowers in the season. I saw here, last summer, some double violets as large as small pinks, and the lady of the house was kind enough to give me some of the roots.

WILLIAM COBBETT,
Rural Rides, 1822

This is Buckinghamshire.

Chesham is a nice little town, lying in a deep and narrow valley, with a stream of water running through it. All along the country that I have come, the labourers' dwellings are good. They are made of what they call *brick-nog* . . . and you see here, as in Kent, Sussex, Surrey and Hampshire, and, indeed, in almost every part of England, that most interesting of all objects, that which is such an honour to England, and that which distinguishes it from all the rest of the world, namely, those *neatly kept and productive little gardens round the labourers' houses,* which are seldom unornamented with more or less of flowers. We have only to look at these to know what sort of people English labourers are: these gardens are the answer to the *Malthuses* and the *Scarletts.* Shut your mouths, you Scotch economists; cease balling, Mr Brougham, and you Edinburgh Reviewers, till *you* can show us something . . . of *this*!

WILLIAM COBBETT,
Rural Rides, 1822

This is Oxfordshire.

They grew all the sweet old-fashioned cottage garden flowers, pinks
and sweet williams and love-in-a-mist, wallflowers and forget-me-
nots in spring and hollyhocks and Michaelmas daisies in autumn.
Then there were lavender and sweetbriar bushes, and southernwood,
sometimes called 'lad's love', but known there as 'old man'.

Almost every garden had its rose bush; but there were no coloured
roses among them. Only Old Sally had those; the other people had
to be content with that meek, old-fashioned white rose with a pink
flush at the heart known as the 'maiden's blush' . . .

As well as their flower garden, the women cultivated a herb
corner, stocked with thyme and parsley and sage for cooking,
rosemary to flavour the home-made lard, lavender to scent the best
clothes, and peppermint, pennyroyal, horehound, camomile, tansy,
balm, and rue for physic.

FLORA THOMPSON,
Lark Rise to Candleford, 1939

In the north of England, standards were lower. Mrs Gaskell, who lived
most of her life in or near Manchester, is an impeccable witness.

At that time gardening was not a popular art in any part of England;
in the north it is not yet. Noblemen and gentlemen may have
beautiful gardens; but farmers and day-labourers care little for them
north of the Trent, which is all I can answer for. A few 'berry'
bushes, a black currant tree or two (the leaves to be used in
heightening the flavour of tea, the fruit as medicinal for colds and
sore throats), a potato ground (and this was not so common at the
close of the last century as it is now), a cabbage bed, a bush of sage,
and balm, and thyme, and marjoram, with possibly a rose tree, and
'old man' growing in the midst; a little plot of small strong coarse
onions, and perhaps some marigolds, the petals of which flavoured
the salt-beef broth; such plants made up a well-furnished garden to
a farmhouse at the time and place to which my story belongs.

MRS GASKELL
Sylvia's Lovers, 1863–4

Too much sweetness cloys, but luckily there are plenty of angry gardening writers to redress the balance. Pope never pulled his punches.

> At Timon's Villa let us pass a day,
> Where all cry out, 'What sums are thrown away!'
> So proud, so grand, of that stupendous air,
> Soft and Agreeable come never there . . .
> His gardens next your admiration call,
> On ev'ry side you look, behold the wall!
> No pleasing intricacies intervene,
> No artful wildness to perplex the scene;
> Grove nods at grove, each alley has a brother,
> And half the platform just reflects the other.
> The suff'ring eye inverted nature sees,
> Trees cut to statues, statues thick as trees,
> With here a fountain, never to be play'd,
> And there a summer-house, that knows no shade.

ALEXANDER POPE,
An Epistle to Lord Burlington, 1731

William Robinson was a past master of invective.

Mowing the grass once a fortnight in pleasure grounds, as now practised, is a costly mistake. We want shaven carpets of grass here and there, but what nonsense it is to shave it as often as foolish men shave their faces! There are indeed places where men boast of mowing forty acres! Who would not rather see the waving grass with countless flowers than a close surface without a blossom? Think of the labour wasted in this ridiculous work of cutting the heads of flowers and grass. Let much of the grass grow till fit to cut for hay, and we may enjoy in it a world of lovely flowers that will blossom and perfect their growth before hay time. Some who have carried out the ideas of this book have waving lawns of feathery grass where they used to shave the grass every ten days; a cloud of flowers where a daisy was not let to peep.

WILLIAM ROBINSON,
The Wild Garden (1870),
1894 edition

Nor are all gardeners sweet-tempered people. Walter Savage Landor was eccentric, irascible, even violent at times, beloved by many, but notorious for his wild behaviour. He lived for some years on the heights of Fiesole, above Florence, where he had a beautiful garden with a violet bed. Lord Houghton records:

The Florentine legend was that he had one day, after an imperfect dinner, thrown the cook out of the window, and, while the man was writhing with a broken limb, ejaculated 'Good God! I forgot the violets.'

RICHARD MONCKTON MILNES, LORD HOUGHTON,
Monographs, 1873

In the top echelons of gardening and botany, the Scots have always won renown. But they have not always come up to the mark as employees.

I am sensibly obliged, my dear Lord, by your great goodness, and am most disposed to take the gardener you recommend, if I can. You are so good-natured you will not blame my suspense. I have a gardener that has lived with me above twenty-five years; he is incredibly ignorant, and a mule. When I wrote to your Lordship, my patience was worn out, and I resolved at least to have a gardener for flowers. On your not being able to give me one, I half consented to keep my own; not on his amendment, but because he will not leave me, presuming on my long suffering. I have offered him fifteen pounds a year to leave me, and when he pleads that he is old, and that nobody else will take him, I plead that I am old too, and that it is rather hard that I am not to have a few flowers, or a little fruit as long as I live. I shall now try if I can make any compromise with him, for I own I cannot bear to turn him adrift, nor will starve an old servant, though never a good one, to please my nose and mouth. Besides, he is a Scot, and I will not be unjust, even to that odious nation; and the more I dislike him, the less will I allow my partiality to persuade me I am in the right . . . I will take the liberty of letting you know, if I can persuade the Serpent that has reduced my little Eden to be as nasty and barren as the Highlands, to take a pension and a yellow ribbon.

But Walpole never got his new gardener. Ten years later, the Scot was still with him, ruining the carnations.

HORACE WALPOLE
to the Earl of Harcourt, 1777,
Letters, Vol. VI

That excellent pig-loving peer, Lord Emsworth, was another who was troubled by a Scots gardener. He was frankly terrified of Angus McAllister, who did what he liked and would not allow his lordship to pick a flower.

The morning sunshine descended like an amber showerbath on Blandings Castle, lighting up with a heartening glow its ivied walls, its rolling parks, its gardens, outhouses, and messuages, and such of its inhabitants as chanced at the moment to be taking the air. It fell on green lawns and wide terraces, on noble trees and bright flowerbeds. It fell on the baggy trousers-seat of Angus McAllister, head-gardener to the ninth Earl of Emsworth, as he bent with dour Scottish determination to pluck a slug from its reverie beneath the leaf of a lettuce . . .

It would be idle to deny that those gardens contained flarze in full measure. They were bright with Achillea, Bignonia Radicans, Campanula, Digitalis, Euphorbia, Funkia, Gypsophila, Helianthus, Iris, Liatris, Monarda, Phlox Drummondi, Salvia, Thalictrum, Vinca and Yucca. But the devil of it was that Angus McAllister would have a fit if they were picked.

P. G. WODEHOUSE,
Blandings Castle

Cobbett accused the Scots of being positively lazy.

It is curious to observe how the different labours are divided as to the *nations*. The mowers are all *English*; the haymakers all *Irish*. Scotchmen toil hard enough in Scotland; but when they go from home it is not to *work*, if you please. They are found in gardens, and especially in gentlemen's gardens. Tying up flowers, picking dead leaves off exotics, peeping into melon-frames, publishing the banns of marriage between the '*male*' and '*female*' blossoms, tap-tap-tapping against a wall with a hammer that weighs half an ounce. They have backs as straight and shoulders as square as heroes of Waterloo; and who can blame them? The digging, the mowing, the carting of loads; all the back-break and sweat-extracting work they leave to be performed by those who have less *prudence* than they have.

WILLIAM COBBETT,
Rural Rides, 1822

Every season of the year has its own charm for those who love gardens. I have chosen a summer verse from Matthew Arnold, an appreciation of winter by Vita Sackville-West.

Too quick despairer, wherefore wilt thou go?
  Soon will the high Midsummer pomps come on,
    Soon will the musk carnations break and swell,
  Soon shall we have gold-dusted snapdragon,
    Sweet-William with its homely cottage smell,
      And stocks in fragrant blow;
  Roses that down the alleys shine afar,
    And open, jasmine muffled lattices,
    And groups under the dreaming garden trees,
  And the full moon, and the white evening-star.

MATTHEW ARNOLD,
a verse from *Thyrsis*, 1867

Then may you shoulder spade and hoe
And heavy-booted homeward go,
For no new flowers shall be born
Save hellebore on Christmas morn,
And bare gold jasmine on the wall,
And violets, and soon the small
Blue netted iris, like a cry
Startling the sloth of February.

V. SACKVILLE-WEST,
The Land, 1926

Most of us feel from time to time that our garden is a lunatic asylum. Of twelve plants in a row, ten come up perfectly and two opt out. Or a nice round shrub decides to grow sideways. Or a winter plant develops a habit of blooming in July. We bear it as best we can. But Mr Bowles collected eccentric plants and made a special home for them which he called the Lunatic Asylum.

In the days of my early youth a vast clump, or so it then seemed to me, of evergreens occupied the space which now forms my home for demented plants. It was the sort of planting one sees at one end of a London square. Portugal Laurels there were, and the still more objectionable Common Laurel; Laurustinus bushes, which in showery weather exhale an odour of dirty dog-kennel and an even dirtier dog; leprously spotted Aucubas and Privet jostled one another round the feet of two Weymouth Pines and a dead Yew covered with Ivy, the whole dismal crew being rendered more awful and uninteresting by having all their attempts to show any beauty that might be inherent in their natural manner of growth nipped in the bud by the garden shears . . . Most of this has now been cleared away . . . Then a home was needed for some trees and shrubs of abnormal characteristics that I had been collecting, and the Lunatic Asylum sprang into existence.

The twisted Hazel was the first crazy occupant, and is perhaps the maddest of all even now. It was first found in a hedge by Lord Ducie, near Tortworth, who moved it into the garden, increased it by layering, and so distributed it to a few friends, my plant being a sucker given me by Canon Ellacombe from his fine specimen. It is a most remarkable form, for it never produces a bit of straight wood; the stem between each leaf is curved as though one side had grown much faster than the other, and alternating lengths are generally curved in opposite directions; frequently they are twisted spirally as well, so that the whole bush is a collection of various curves and spirals, a tangle of crooks and corkscrews from root to tip . . . A young plant of a similarly twisted Hawthorn has now come to be a companion to the nut, but has not had time to develop its mania very fully. As a contrast there is the fastigiate form of the common Elder, the wood of which grows as stiff and straight and upright as a grenadier . . .

Yet another Elder has been certified insane and admitted to this select company. Its madness consists in the greater portion of the lamina of the leaf blades being reduced to a mere thread, and it looks as though an army of locusts or caterpillars had halted to dine on it, but for all that has rather a soft, ferny look from a distance.

Two Laburnums have developed strange habits, and qualified for admittance: one pretends to be an Oak, and has, so far as it can, imitated its leaves, and the name of *quercifolium* has been added to its own of *Laburnum vulgare*. The flowers are of a good rich yellow, but of course turn to ordinary pods, not acorns. The second is var. *involutum*, and has every leaflet rolled inward, giving the whole tree a heavy, congested appearance, and at close quarters one would think the leaves must be full of green fly to be so much rolled up.

E. A. BOWLES,
My Garden in Spring, 1914

What is a delight to one generation of gardeners is a freak to the next — one man's cherub is another man's gnome. Sometimes the divergence of taste is a matter, not of generation, but of social standing. Pope's bête noire *was topiary, beloved of gardeners in the late seventeenth century. He wrote a spoof catalogue of topiary available from the nurseries.*

Adam and Eve in yew; Adam a little shattered by the fall of the Tree of Knowledge in the great storm; Eve and the serpent very flourishing.

The Tower of Babel, not yet finished.

St George in box; his arm scarce long enough, but will be in a condition to stick the dragon by next April.

A green dragon of the same, with a tail of ground-ivy for the present.

N.B. These two not to be sold separately.

Edward the Black Prince in cypress.

A laurustine bear in blossom, with a juniper hunter in Berries.

A pair of giants, stunted, to be sold cheap . . .

An old Maid of Honour in wormwood.

A topping Ben Jonson in laurel.

ALEXANDER POPE,
The Guardian, 1713

Walpole, though an ardent practitioner of the Picturesque, was crisp about its absurder fantasies.

The ornament whose merit soonest fades is the hermitage or scene adapted to contemplation. It is almost comic to set aside a quarter of one's garden to be melancholy in.

HORACE WALPOLE,
On Modern Gardening, 1770 (published 1780)

Miss Jekyll abominated the dwarfing of flowers. It is a mercy she did not live to see our horrible dwarf hollyhocks and foxgloves, her nightmare realized.

No annual plant has of late years been so much improved as the Sweet Pea, and one reason why its charming beauty and scent are so enjoyable is, that they grow tall, and can be seen on a level with the eye. There can be no excuse whatever for dwarfing this, as has been lately done. There are already plenty of good flowering plants under a foot high, and the little dwarf white monstrosity, now being followed by coloured ones of the same habit, seems to me worthy of nothing but condemnation. It would be as right and sensible to dwarf a Hollyhock into a podgy mass a foot high, or a Penstemon, or a Foxglove.

GERTRUDE JEKYLL,
Wood and Garden, 1899

Let us now put aside all peevish thoughts, and forget incompetent gardeners,
acrimonious theories, ostentatious statues, snobbish visitors, disgusting pests
and hostile weather, and end with pure garden delight. Some gardeners find
most pleasure in luxuriant flowers and fruit, others in fine vegetables, some
in the search for new garden flowers, others in the companionship of birds,
and many love a garden for its tranquillity. Henry Austin Dobson's little
garden prospers like the ever-fruiting garden of Alcinous.

Here in this sequester'd close
Bloom the hyacinth and rose,
Here beside the modest stock
Flaunts the flaring hollyhock;
Here, without a pang, one sees
Ranks, conditions and degrees.

All the seasons run their race
In this quiet resting place;
Peach and apricot and fig
Here will ripen and grow big;
Here is store and overplus, —
More had not Alcinous.

HENRY AUSTIN DOBSON,
At the Sign of the Lyre, 1885

Lady Granville, a delightful letter-writer, loved a kitchen garden. She rushed to the potager *when visiting Trentham, seat of Lord Stafford, to admire its perfect cultivation.*

They were out when we came. I rushed to the *potager* — you know my weakness — and walked up and down between spinach and dahlias in ecstasy.

This is in many ways a beautiful place and the *tenue*, the neatness, the training of flowers and fruit trees, gates, enclosures, hedges, are what in no other country is dreamt of; and then there is a repose, a *laisser aller*, a freedom, and a security in a *vie de château* that no other destiny offers one. I feel when I set out to walk as if alone in the world — nothing but trees and birds; but then comes the enormous satisfaction of always finding a man dressing a hedge, or a woman in a gingham and a black bonnet on her knees picking up weeds, the natural gendarmerie of the country, and the most comfortable well-organized country.

HARRIET, COUNTESS GRANVILLE,
letters to her sister, Lady Carlisle, 1828

Reginald Farrer found ecstasy in collecting for gardens thousands of miles from home. His companion in north-west China in 1914 was William Purdom.

Suddenly upon the brink of a crumbling cliff I heard Purdom give the alarm; and joining him, was driven frantic by the most beautiful of small bushes that sprouted inaccessible from its face. It was our first sight of *Dipelta elegans*, that rivals *Viburnum fragrans* in grace of habit and the charm of its abundant blossom . . . It made one jump to see it, its boughs bending beneath their burden of swollen-throated five-lipped bells of a softest pearly-white or faintest shell-pink, with a reticulation on the lower lip of what seemed like orange velvet . . . It subsequently, in its full splendour, gave us many hours of solemn rapture in its Tibetan home.

REGINALD FARRER,
On the Eaves of the World, 1917

Thomas Hardy found pleasure in sharing his cottage garden with his friends, the birds.

When the inmate stirs, the birds retire discreetly
From the window-ledge, whereon they whistled sweetly
    And on the step of the door,
     In the misty morning hoar;
   But now the dweller is up they flee
   To the crooked neighbouring codlin-tree;
And when he comes fully forth they seek the garden,
And call from the lofty costard, as pleading pardon
    For shouting so near before
    In their joy at being alive: —
Meanwhile the hammering clock within goes five.

I know a domicile of brown and green,
Where for a hundred summers there have been
Just such enactments, just such daybreaks seen.

THOMAS HARDY,
A Bird-Scene at a Rural Dwelling

*The loveliest garden poem of all, and perhaps the best known, is by Andrew
Marvell. Full of imagery and symbolism, its meaning has to be teased out,
and is different for every reader. Some stress its irony, some the deeper ideas
suggested by each symbol, but at first reading, at least, it can be taken more
simply: the poet contrasts the strivings of the ambitious townsman with a
country paradise where man can retreat into the world of his imagination.*

> How vainly men themselves amaze
> To win the palm, the oak, or bays;
> And their uncessant labours see
> Crown'd from some single herb or tree,
> Whose short and narrow verged shade
> Does prudently their toils upbraid;
> While all flow'rs and all trees do close
> To weave the garlands of repose . . .
>
> What wond'rous life is this I lead!
> Ripe apples drop about my head;
> The luscious clusters of the vine
> Upon my mouth do crush their wine;
> The nectarine, and curious peach,
> Into my hands themselves do reach;
> Stumbling on melons, as I pass,
> Insnar'd with flowers, I fall on grass.
>
> Meanwhile the mind, from pleasure less,
> Withdraws into its happiness:
> The mind, that ocean where each kind
> Does streight its own resemblance find;
> Yet it creates, transcending these,
> Far other world, and other seas,
> Annihilating all that's made
> To a green thought in a green shade.

ANDREW MARVELL,
three verses from *The Garden c.* 1650

The last word must be with Voltaire.

'I, also, know,' said Candide, 'that we must cultivate our garden.'

'You are right,' said Pangloss, 'for when man was put into the Garden of Eden, he was put there to work, which proves that man was not born to be idle.'

'Let us work, then, without arguing,' said Martin; 'it is the only way of making life bearable.'

The little society, one and all, entered into this laudable scheme; each one set himself to use his talents. The little piece of ground bore plentifully. Cunégonde was in truth very ugly, but she became an excellent pastry-cook; Pacquette embroidered; the old woman looked after the linen. There was none, down to Brother Giroflée, but did some service; he was a very good carpenter, and so became an honest man; and Pangloss would sometimes say to Candide:

'All events are linked in a chain in the best of all possible worlds; for, when all is said and done, if you had not been kicked out of a fine castle by the backside for the love of Mlle Cunégonde, if you had not been a victim of the Inquisition, if you had not chased over America on foot, if you had not struck the Baron with your sword, if you had not lost all the sheep you brought from the good country of Eldorado, you would not be here eating preserved fruit and pistachio nuts.'

'That is well said,' answered Candide, 'but we must cultivate our garden.'

VOLTAIRE,
Candide, 1758

── ACKNOWLEDGEMENTS ──

Thanks are due to the following authors, copyright owners, and publishers for permission to reprint the following pieces and extracts:

EDGAR BATEMAN: *If it wasn't for the 'ouses in between (The Cockney's Garden)*, © 1894 Francis Day & Hunter Ltd. Reproduced by permission of E.M.I. Music Publishing Ltd.

E. F. BENSON: Extract from *Mapp and Lucia* reprinted by permission of the Executors of the Estate of the late K. S. P. McDowell and William Heinemann Limited.

JOHN BETJEMAN: The poem 'Pot Pourri from a Surrey Garden' from *Collected Poems* published by John Murray (Publishers) Ltd. Reprinted by permission of the publishers.

AMBROSE BIERCE: Extract from *The Enlarged Devil's Dictionary* published by Victor Gollancz Ltd and Doubleday. Reprinted by permission of the publishers.

WILFRID BLUNT: Extract from *A Gardener's Dozen* reprinted by kind permission of the author and B.B.C. Publications. Extract from *Tulipomania* (King Penguin, 1950) pp. 15–16. Copyright 1950 Wilfrid Blunt. Reprinted by permission of Penguin Books Ltd and the author.

MAUREEN AND BRIDGET BOLAND: Extracts from *Old Wives' Lore for Gardeners* reprinted by permission of the publishers, The Bodley Head.

E. A. BOWLES: Extracts from *My Garden in Spring* reprinted by permission of Thomas Nelson and Sons Ltd.

ROBERT BYRON: Extract from *The Road to Oxiana*, published by Jonathan Cape Ltd, reprinted by permission of A. D. Peters & Co. Ltd.

KAREL ČAPEK: Extracts from *The Gardener's Year*, published by George Allen & Unwin (Publishers) Ltd, reprinted by permission of the publishers.

JOHN CAREY: Extracts from 'The Pleasures of Vegetable Gardening' from *The Sunday Times* of 24 February 1980 reprinted by permission of the author and *The Sunday Times*.

'CASSANDRA': Article entitled 'A Ray of Sunshine' copyright Daily Mirror/Syndication International. Reprinted by permission of Syndication International Ltd.

BETH CHATTO: Extract from *The Damp Garden*, published by J. M. Dent & Sons Ltd, reprinted by permission of the author and of the publisher.

GEOFFREY CHAUCER: 20 lines from *The Nun's Priest's Tale* from *The Canterbury Tales*, translated into modern English by Nevill Coghill (Penguin Classics, revised edition, 1977), pp. 232, 233. Copyright 1951 by Nevill Coghill. Copyright © Nevill Coghill, 1958, 1960, 1975, 1977. Reprinted by permission of Penguin Books Ltd.

COLETTE: Extracts from *Sido* from *My Mother's House* and *Sido* translated by Enid McLeod, reprinted by permission of Martin Secker & Warburg Limited. *Extrait de COLETTE: SIDO*, Hachette, Editeur, Paris.

CYRIL CONNOLLY: Extract from *Horizon*, December 1949–January 1950 and inscription in book sent to Lady Glenconner reprinted by kind permission of Mrs Deirdre Levi.

MARGERY FISH: Extract from *A Flower for Every Day*, 1965, Studio Vista, reprinted by permission of Macmillan Publishing Co., Inc. and Mr Francis Boyd-Carpenter.

E. M. FORSTER: Extract from *A Passage to India*, published by Edward Arnold (Publishers) Ltd, reprinted by permission of the publishers.

ANDRÉ GIDE: Extracts from *The Journals of André Gide*, translated by Justin O'Brien. Copyright 1947, 1948 by Alfred A. Knopf, Inc. Reprinted by permission of the publisher. Also reprinted by permission of Martin Secker & Warburg Limited.

DR D. G. HESSAYON: Extract from *Be Your Own Vegetable Doctor*, pbi Publications 1978, reprinted by permission of the publishers.

RALPH HODGSON: The poem 'The Rose' from *Collected Poems* by Ralph Hodgson, reprinted by permission of Mrs Ralph Hodgson and Macmillan, London and Basingstoke.

ANTHONY HUXLEY: Approx. 220 words from *Plant and Planet* (Allen Lane, 1974), p. 247. Copyright © Anthony Huxley, 1974. Reprinted by permission of Penguin Books Ltd and the author.

RUDYARD KIPLING: Three verses from 'The Glory of the Garden'. Reprinted by permission of The National Trust.

LAURIE LEE: Extract from *Cider with Rosie*, published by Chatto & Windus, reprinted by permission of the publishers.

BERNARD LEVIN: Extract from *Taking Sides*, published by Jonathan Cape Ltd, reprinted by permission of the author. Extract from article in *The Times*, 11 April 1974, reprinted by permission of the author.

CHRISTOPHER LLOYD: Extracts from *The Well Tempered Garden*, 1970, published by Wm Collins Sons & Co., reprinted by permission of the author and publisher.

OSBERT SITWELL: Extract from *Sing High! Sing Low!*, published by Gerald Duckworth & Co. Ltd, reprinted by permission of the publishers.

ROY STRONG: Excerpt from an interview given to Anne Scott-James, printed in *Harpers & Queen*, February 1974. Reprinted by permission of Sir Roy Strong and *Harpers & Queen*.

DYLAN THOMAS: Extract from *Under Milk Wood*, published by J. M. Dent & Sons Ltd. Reprinted by permission of David Higham Associates Limited.

FLORA THOMPSON: Extracts from *Lark Rise to Candleford* (1954), reprinted by permission of Oxford University Press.

ALICE B. TOKLAS: Extract from *The Alice B. Toklas Cook Book*, published by Michael Joseph Ltd. Reprinted by permission of the publishers.

FRANK KINGDON WARD: Extract from *The Romance of Plant Hunting*, published by Edward Arnold (Publishers) Ltd. Reprinted by permission of the publishers and A. D. Peters & Co. Ltd. Extract from *Plant Hunting on the Edge of the World*, published by Victor Gollancz Ltd. Reprinted by permission of A. D. Peters & Co. Ltd.

P. G. WODEHOUSE: Extracts from *Blandings Castle* and *Lord Emsworth and Others* reprinted by permission of Lady Ethel Wodehouse and the Hutchinson Group Ltd.

Two letters to *Popular Gardening* are reprinted here by permission of the magazine.

INDEX OF AUTHORS

INDEX OF EXTRACTS

FOR THE BEST IN PAPERBACKS, LOOK FOR THE

In every corner of the world, on every subject under the sun, Penguin represents quality and variety – the very best in publishing today.

For complete information about books available from Penguin – including Pelicans, Puffins, Peregrines and Penguin Classics – and how to order them, write to us at the appropriate address below. Please note that for copyright reasons the selection of books varies from country to country.

In the United Kingdom: For a complete list of books available from Penguin in the U.K., please write to *Dept E.P., Penguin Books Ltd, Harmondsworth, Middlesex, UB7 0DA*

In the United States: For a complete list of books available from Penguin in the U.S., please write to *Dept BA, Penguin, 299 Murray Hill Parkway, East Rutherford, New Jersey 07073*

In Canada: For a complete list of books available from Penguin in Canada, please write to *Penguin Books Canada Ltd, 2801 John Street, Markham, Ontario L3R 1B4*

In Australia: For a complete list of books available from Penguin in Australia, please write to the *Marketing Department, Penguin Books Australia Ltd, P.O. Box 257, Ringwood, Victoria 3134*

In New Zealand: For a complete list of books available from Penguin in New Zealand, please write to the *Marketing Department, Penguin Books (NZ) Ltd, Private Bag, Takapuna, Auckland 9*

In India: For a complete list of books available from Penguin, please write to *Penguin Overseas Ltd, 706 Eros Apartments, 56 Nehru Place, New Delhi, 110019*

In Holland: For a complete list of books available from Penguin in Holland, please write to *Penguin Books Nederland B.V., Postbus 195, NL–1380AD Weesp, Netherlands*

In Germany: For a complete list of books available from Penguin, please write to *Penguin Books Ltd, Friedrichstrasse 10 – 12, D–6000 Frankfurt Main 1, Federal Republic of Germany*

In Spain: For a complete list of books available from Penguin in Spain, please write to *Longman Penguin España, Calle San Nicolas 15, E–28013 Madrid, Spain*

Also by Anne Scott-James in Penguin

THE COTTAGE GARDEN

The story of the cottage garden – with its herbs and honeysuckle and its pig in the sty – from Chaucer's time until today.

'The kind of scholarship and personal experience which fires recollection . . . a wise summary of one of our finest national accomplishments' – Ronald Blythe

'Delightful . . . witty and fluent' – *Irish Times*

'Her history is neatly and simply laid out; well-stocked with attractive illustrations, paintings, drawings and engravings' – Francis Gibb in *The Times*

'A joy to read, look at and dip into . . . the perfect present' – *Woman's Journal*

'Any gardener who aspires to more than just growing things, might go a long way towards making an idyllic small garden after reading this book' – *Evening Standard*